For my parents:

T. Noel Osborn

Georgia Bagnetto Osborn

This book is the first
Inter-American Studies
published by
The Center for Inter-American Studies
and
Texas Western Press
The University of Texas at El Paso
79968

HIGHER
IN

GULF OF CALIFORNIA

SONORA

CHIHUAHUA

COAHU

DURANGO

ZACATECA

S

AGUAS-
CALIENT

SINALOA

NAYARIT

JALISCO

COLIMA

MICH

0	50	100		200	MILES
0		100	200	300	KILOMETERS

Map by Stephen N. Harden

EDUCATION
MEXICO

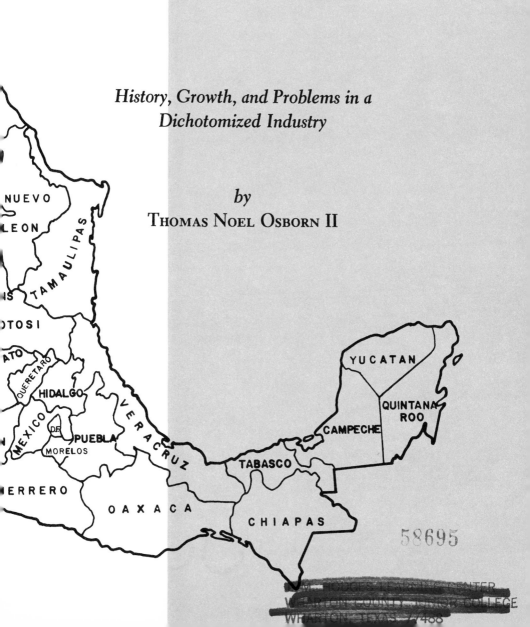

*History, Growth, and Problems in a
Dichotomized Industry*

by
THOMAS NOEL OSBORN II

Designed by

EVAN HAYWOOD ANTONE

PREFACE

 THE PRESENT BOOK is primarily intended for two audiences, U.S. scholars interested in Mexican higher education, and Mexican scholars and decision-makers who are part of that system and are directly affected by the implications of the analysis herein. The first group will see in the history and description of the Mexican educational system some interesting contrasts — and parallels — with the development of their own. It is hoped that this group will turn more attention to the interesting and analyzable problems in educational systems such as the Mexican one, where their expertise and experience would be of great value in identifying and examining pressing problems in the development of human capital resources.

For the second group, I would hope that this work provides not only a basis for further research, but also a challenge to attack the problems posed by the rapid growth of the Mexican university system and the need for higher quality throughout.

Unfortunately, although the Mexican university has frequently been an amphitheater for sounding out national problems, it has not traditionally been the place where scholars have united to help solve these problems. Many of the best human resources in the country have been drawn into industry and government, and these entities have absorbed the energies of even those scholars who have lent their services on a part-time basis to the university. Research in general, and research into social-science problems in particular, has not been the forte of the Mexican university. I sincerely hope that this book serves as a stimulus to university educators and administrators to take the leadership in the search for creative solutions to the problems discussed herein. It must be clear to Mexico's *universitarios*, that if they do not research the problems of higher education and human capital formation and attempt to solve them from within the university system, they can expect that solutions will be imposed upon them from outside.

To other readers, particularly those of the Third World countries, I would suggest that the Mexican model of higher education serves to illuminate some of the problems to be faced under rapid growth of population and income. Mexico leads many other countries in growth statistics, and although many of the characteristics of her higher educational system are uniquely Mexican, there are others common to any country under development. Therefore, I believe this book has a value beyond the specific institutional framework described.

As with any author, I have assumed many debts in the preparation of this book. In its original form, the book was my doctoral dissertation, researched and written while I was a Visiting Professor of Economics at the Autonomous University of Guadalajara. This opportunity was made possible by grants under the Fulbright-Hays Act and from the Rockefeller Foundation and the University of Colorado. Special thanks are due to Wyn F. Owen, Director of the Economics Institute and the International Economic Studies Center of the University of Colorado, who was responsible for opening the opportunity to me and without whose guidance and encouragement over the years this book would never have been completed. The manuscript was finished while I was a Fulbright Professor at the National University of Mexico. For their continued assistance and support I would like to thank the officials of the Cultural Section, U.S. Embassy, Mexico, and of the Bureau of Educational and Cultural Affairs, U.S. State Department, Washington, and the Board of Foreign Scholarships.

Many others were of considerable help along the way. The officials of the universities I interviewed gave most generously of their time and attention, even though they were genuinely busy with the many problems of running their own institutions. Lic. Jesús Barrón of the National Association of Universities (ANUIES) was most helpful in making university data available and clarifying difficult points. My understanding of the Mexican educational system has benefited from countless discussions with my students and colleages at the Autonomous University of Guadalajara and the National University of Mexico. The staff of the Economics and Business Research Center of the AUG provided a sounding board for the consideration of many of the problems raised in the analysis.

For their splendid insights and comments I would like to thank Professor Carl McGuire of the University of Colorado, Dr. Manuel Servín of the National Council of Science and Technology (CONACYT), Ing. Carlos Gómez Figueroa of ANUIES, and Professors Charles Richter of the National Polytechnic Institute and Roberto Newell of the University of the Americas. Although spouses always share the burden and the joy of an author's work, my wife Dede's participation went above and beyond the call of duty many times and in many ways.

Whatever flaws exist in this work are, of course, the exclusive property of this author, who, although he is an outsider looking in, hopes he is contributing to the formation of human capital in a country which has always been a most courteous host.

THOMAS NOEL OSBORN II

Mexico City
January, 1976

CONTENTS

LIST OF TABLES

HIGHER EDUCATION IN MEXICO

I : INTRODUCTION

THE ECONOMICS OF EDUCATION has become a most important subject in economic literature in recent years. Its importance derives in part from the fact that the "product" of the educational process is tied so closely to the concept of the development of human capital. Moreover, the education "industry" is quite a peculiar animal in itself, different in many ways from other industries absorbing material and human resources as inputs. As Mark Blaug has written:

> . . . in most countries, [education] is largely collectively provided and financed; although the inputs of teachers and buildings are bought in the market place, the output of students is not sold; its production cycle is longer that that of most other industries and it consumes a relatively large fraction of its own output; it is not a profit-maximising activity and indeed, it is not self-evident that it is maximising anything at all; it is both "investment" and "consumption" in so far as it prepares students both to earn a living and to enjoy the fruits of living; its pay-off takes a long time to materialize but it depreciates slowly and rarely becomes entirely obsolete; it serves to diffuse the existing stock of knowledge but it also acts to increase that stock; it both preserves and disseminates social values, sometimes fostering and sometimes impeding social and occupational mobility; its economic consequences are complex and so thoroughly intertwined with its social and political effects that any hope of separating them can be made to seem absurd.[1]

This study cannot hope to handle all or even most of the problem areas in Blaug's list, even for one country, but it will hope to touch upon several of them. The following chapters will attempt to present some measures of the scope and outreach of Mexico's education effort, touching on how this effort compares with that of some other countries, particularly Latin ones. Special attention will be devoted to the public finance aspects of education because in Mexico it is true that education is " . . . largely collectively provided and financed," and included in the public sector. Nevertheless, an important private sector does exist, particularly in higher education, and some of the differences between public and private sector universities will be detailed.

A basic problem which this study attacks is that of the finance of private higher education in Mexico. It will be seen that a dichotomy between public and private sectors with regard to higher education results in an almost total lack of public funding for private universities. This situation is not in harmony with the private universities' importance to the Mexican educational structure, nor with the need for increased "publicness" among the private universities as they respond to a fast-growing demand for educational services. The scope and nature of this problem is presented herein, and an attempt to find solutions that are consistent in a Mexican context is begun.

Very little has been done for Mexico in this area or in the other areas identified by Blaug in the economics of education. A pioneering effort in the area of education's effect on the economic growth of the country has been written by Charles Nash Myers;[2] and the literature has also been enriched by Martin Carnoy's research on the rates of return to education in Mexico.[3] In the Mexican literature in Spanish, a wealth of material is available on the historical, social, cultural, and political facets of education, but very little on economic aspects. Some interesting work on resource allocation at all levels of education and manpower planning has been done by the Centro de Estudios Educativos, A. C., formerly under the direction of Pablo Latapí, a leading Mexican educator.[4]

With regard to higher education, there is a void of published material in English or in Spanish dealing with the economics of the Mexican university. Probably the only attempt so far to describe contemporary Mexican universities in an organized way has been done by Richard King,[5] an American educator. King, with the help of the Mexican educator Alfonso Rangel Guerra and others of the International Council for Educational Development, has written a seminal work describing the provincial universities of Mexico and relating their strengths and problems to regional needs. King is not an economist, however, and although his comments on the financing of the provincial universities are quite helpful, his focus is not on the economics of the universities of his sample nor on the public-private nexus. King's analysis will be examined in the course of this book, and an attempt will be made to deal in economic terms with one of King's issues, that of quality in education.

It will be necessary to begin with a sketch of Mexican history, as that history bears upon the development of educational infrastructure. As Raymond Vernon warns:

Anyone who attemps to understand contemporary Mexico without much reference to its history courts major risks. This is certainly true of any effort to understand relations between the public and the private sectors in Mexico.[6]

Since the present study will spotlight these very relations, Chapter Two's historical review will be essential to understand what follows.

In Chapter Three some of the characteristics of Mexican universities are measured, with particular reference to the size of the institutions and their distribution throughout the country. A first distinction between public and private universities is drawn on the basis of size. In addition, some characteristics of the "typical" university student are described.

Chapter Four separates further the public and private sectors in higher education and outlines recent growth trends in each sector. Most of the chapter is concerned with educational quality between the two sectors.

Chapter Five projects ahead the demand for higher education in Mexico, and the cost of that education. The chapter then relates the private universities to these projections, with an attempt to evaluate the elasticity of private university income sources.

The data base for much of the present study is the now-annual series of the National Association of Universities and Institutes of Higher Learning (*Asociación Nacional de Universidades e Institutos de Enseñanza Superior* - ANUIES), a semi-official government organization which serves as a clearing house for information from the Mexican institutions of higher learning, particularly the public institutions. Since 1966 a considerable amount of information is available for all universities, even though the private institutions have been traditionally reluctant to report. Year by year the data and its organization is improved.

Information on the private universities was augmented by interviews with administrators at ten selected private institutions during the Spring and Fall of 1972. These universities were chosen on the basis of their location, size, prestige, and an evaluation of their overall "importance" on a subjective basis. The universities included were: Monterrey Technological Institute (Instituto Tecnológico y de Estudios Superiores de Monterrey); Autonomous University of Guadalajara (Universidad Autónoma de Guadalajara); Autonomous Technological Institute of Mexico (Instituto Tecnológico Autónomo de México); Iberoamerican University (Universidad Iberoamericana); Technological University of Mexico (Universidad Tecnológica de México); Higher Institute for Commercial Studies (Instituto Superior de Estudios Comerciales); Anáhuac University (Universidad Anáhuac); Women's University of Mexico (Universidad Femenina de México); University of the Valley of Mexico (Universidad del Valle de México — formerly Harvard Institution); La Salle University (Universidad La Salle). All of these institutions made information available, in varying degrees of completeness, and the first six were able to answer all the questions asked. The basic questionnaire used in the interviews is included as Appendix A. The information concerning the universities that is contained in this book is not limited to the questionnaire, however. Much additional background material was gathered in interviews and relationships with university officials, professors, and students during the five-year period in which the author has taught in private and public Mexican universities.

REFERENCES:

1 Mark Blaug, *Economics of Education: A Selected Annotated Bibliography*, 1970, p. ix.

2 C. N. Myers, *Education and National Development in Mexico*, 1965.

3 See his "Earnings and Schooling in Mexico," in *Economic Development and Cultural Change*, July 1967, and also "Rates of Return to Schooling in Latin America," in *Journal of Human Resources*, Summer 1967.

4 See, for example, the Center's *Diagnóstico Educativo Nacional*, 1964, for a level-by-level analysis of educational developments between 1958 and 1963.

5 Richard King, *The Provincial Universities of Mexico*, 1971.

6 Raymond Vernon, ed., *Public Policy and Private Enterprise in Mexico*, 1964, p. 2.

II : MEXICAN EDUCATIONAL STRUCTURES, HISTORY AND OVERVIEW

ALTHOUGH IT IS NOT REALLY NECESSARY to an understanding of the current state of Mexican education to return to the pre-colonial days of the indigenous peoples of Mexico, a panorama of the nation's history since pre-colonial days will be helpful in understanding the current state of her educational system. In this chapter a broad overview of Mexico's historical development is presented, with special reference to the implications of that development on the country's educational infrastructure.

The Pre-Colonial Heritage

It is interesting to note that the Mexico that Spain colonized was not a primitive land with respect to the culture of its inhabitants. The Mayas had had in Yucatan a very advanced civilization by 1200 A.D., a civilization that ". . . approached contemporaneous European cultures in architecture and sculpture, surpassed them in mathematics and astronomy, and may have rivaled them in providing sustenance and public order."[1]

The Aztecs, whose civilization was in full flourish in Central Mexico when Hernán Cortés began his conquest in 1519, were not far behind the Mayas. The Aztecs possessed a high level of technical skill, economic security, and a culture mature enough to appreciate art and beauty. They too had a stable political system and a capitol city probably as large as Seville, Spain's largest city at the time.[2]

Thus, the colonizers of Mexico, in introducing their legal, political, and intellectual framework into Spanish America, did not build upon a vacuum. Of course, this is not to say that modern or even colonial institutions resemble or are extensions of their indigenous predecessors. But the Indian heritage is strongly felt in Mexico, and it is important to remember that the modern Mexican is a *mestizo*, a mixture between Indian and Spanish,[3] and that at the zenith of Spanish influence, the Spanish and their creole descendents (*criollos*, American-born whites) numbered no more than ten to twenty percent of the population of Mexico.[4] Thus the impact of the Indian and the *mestizo* on Mexican culture cannot be ignored. As one author has pointed out:

While the figure of 10,000,000 is probably an exageration, the fact that there were at least two million or more Indians in early New Spain is highly significant in the explanation of population growth, of land use and management, and of educational policies. The added facts that these people spoke many different tongues, that they were dispersed over a wide extent, in effect were separate nations, are not to be taken lightly in the evaluation of the results which attended the establishment of the European Institutions.[5]

Early Colonial Influences

In any case, the Spanish set out to educate and to Christianize the diverse indigenous groups. This latter aspect is crucial to an understanding of the evolution of education in Mexico since it was carried out in colonial days entirely at the hands of the Church.

The Spanish settlers felt in their duty to bring Christianity to the heathen Indians.[6] Of course, there was much profit to be made along the way. Nevertheless, among the first settlers of Mexico were some very high-principled friars and priests who argued that the conquest could only be justified on religious grounds. It was Catholic Spain's duty to Christianize the Indian, they maintained, and the concomitant exploitation they condemned as a heinous sin.

Among these early religious settlers were such stellar individuals as the Franciscan Pedro de Gante who, in 1523, barely two years after Cortés[7] had subjugated the Aztecs, founded the first school in the Americas—a language school in Texcoco for study of Indian dialects and to teach Spanish to Indian children. Fray Pedro was truly an educational innovator who laid the foundation for education in Mexico during the Colonial period. In about 1526 he took over from Fray Martín de Valencia (who was the superior of the famous Twelve early Franciscans) the renowned Indian school in the San Francisco monastery in Mexico City, the Colegio de San José de Belén de los Naturales.

The Colegio de San José was a remarkable institution for its time. More than an elementary school, it reached out to all age groups and included not only reading, writing, and Latin grammar but also fine arts and music, as well as instruction in such trades as carpentry, tailoring, shoemaking, and stone cutting. Fray Pedro also had the wisdom to use the common Indian language (Nahuatl) in instruction and to include the Indians' ritual singing and dancing in the Catholic services. The Colegio de San José, for its innovativeness and originality, was to become the model for Mexican education at all levels during the colonial period. Summing up his discussion of the Colegio, George Sánchez, a noted Latin American educational authority, has written the following:

The most striking feature of the program was that Fray Pedro and his assistants not only had an eminently sound conception of the psychology of teaching and léarning but they also had a phenomenal insight into the process of acculturation. Because of this, their work presaged the birth of a new, a Mexican culture.[8]

There were other outstanding individuals in the early history of education in the New World. In 1536 the first viceroy of Mexico, Don Antonio de Mendoza, founded and himself endowed an Indian school which was to become the first institution of higher learning in the New World, Santa Cruz de Tlatelolco.[9] Also active in the founding of this college was Juan de Zumárraga, the first bishop of Mexico and official Protector of the Indian. The first rector was thé famous Indian historian, Fray Bernardo de Sahagún, whose monumental work *The History of Things in New Spain* remains today one of the richest sources of information on life in pre-Colombian Mexico.

Unfortunately the Colegio de Santa Cruz fell on hard times, partially due to its own success. It is said that the Spanish were envious of the distinction being attained by the Indian scholars,[10] and also that the College's desires to make priests out of some of its scholars were frowned upon by some influential settlers.[11] In any case, by the end of the 16th century, the college had virtually disappeared.

Another college founded in this period did succeed and remains today a functioning institution. In 1540, Vasco de Quiroga, first Bishop of Michoacán and member of the ruling Audiencia of New Spain, founded the Colegio de San Nicolás Obispo in Pátzcuaro, northwest of Mexico City, for the religious education of both Indians and Spaniards. Later transferred to Valladolid (now Morelia), Michoacán, and renamed San Nicolás de Hidalgo in honor of the father of Mexican independence, the Colegio featured free admission for Spanish, Indian, and *mestizo* young men who wanted to study theology. Today the Colegio de San Nicolás is the preparatory school for the University of Michoacán (Universidad Michoacana de San Nicolás de Hidalgo) and as such stands as the oldest existing institution of higher education in the New World.

Another institution which deserves mention here is the Colegio de San Juan de Letrán, the first school in Mexico created especially for *mestizo* children. Pedro de Gante, Bishop Zumárraga, and Viceroy Mendoza were again responsible for the founding (1547) of the Colegio, which rendered great service to the society until the first part of the 19th century. After the deaths of the founders, the school degenerated somewhat; it continued to serve *mestizo* young people, but it did not receive the support which the realities of the Mexican situation called for nor was its spirit in behalf of the *mestizo* extended in anywhere near the scale necessary. Besides its service to the *mestizo*, the Colegio de San Juan de Letrán is also worthy of note as the first normal school in Mexico, since one of its principal functions was the training of teachers.[12]

But the cornerstone of the edifice of higher education in Mexico during this period was the Royal and Pontifical University of Mexico, which was founded by royal decree in 1551, and which disputes with the University of San Marcos in Lima the distinction of being the oldest university in the New World.[13] Organized after the plan of the University of Salamanca, the University of Mexico was officially opened in 1553 and has served as the most notable university in Mexico for most of the succeeding 400 years of its life.

When founded, the University was in spirit a medieval one, as was the Salamanca institution it was patterned after, and as were the universities of Europe at that time. The methodology of the University and the conduct of its programs was in the scholastic tradition; the defense of dogma was considered superior to the discovery of truth.[14] Nevertheless, courses were offered in Theology, Scripture, Canon Law, Jurisprudence, Arts, Rhetoric, and the Justinian Code. Gradually during the colonial period, other chairs were established in Medicine, and (native) Indian and Oriental Languages. Unfortunately, throughout the colonial period, the University of Mexico retained its medieval character. While other universities in Europe and elsewhere were developing new approaches to learning and were becoming more humanistic, "the University of Mexico continued to remain adverse to the new fields of study and to perpetuate the norms of a by-gone age." [15]

Notwithstanding the traditionalism which would finally lead to its suppression in 1835, the University of Mexico established an enviable educational record during the colonial period. Sánchez notes that by 1636 when the first U.S. university, Harvard College, was founded, the University of Mexico had already *graduated* more than 8,000 students at the bachelor's level (not to say how many other students had attended!). Another author points out, by way of comparison between the University of Mexico and United States universities, that by the year of U.S. independence only nine U.S. colleges had been founded, none of which were truly universities. By that date nearly 1200 doctors' and masters' degrees and fully 30,000 bachelors' degrees had been granted at the University of Mexico, which had then been in continuous operation for 223 years.[16]

There were other noteworthy institutions of higher learning in Mexico during the colonial period. In 1791 the University of Guadalajara was founded, and many celebrated graduates passed through its doors in the thirty years that it fluorished under Spanish rule. Many *colegios* were also established, some of them quite pioneering in their curriculum and methodology. Of special note are the Jesuit institutions, which numbered more than twenty-five by the time the Society was expelled from Mexico in 1767.

Among the Jesuit institutions were some of the most important in Mexico. Mention has already been made of the oldest existing insti-

tution of higher learning in the New World, the Colegio de San Nicolás Obispo, founded by Bishop Vasco de Quiroga in 1540. The
Jesuits took charge of the Colegio in 1573, and that date marks the
beginning of a hundred years of prosperity that attended the institution until the Jesuits withdrew in the late 1600's. In addition, the
Jesuits themselves founded other important institutions. One of the
most notable of these was the Colegio de San Ildefonso which later
(1867) became the National Preparatory School, and which now is
a part of the National University of Mexico.

But more than in sheer numbers, the Jesuits contributed a spirit
of liberal education to New Spain.[17] Before they came to Mexico, higher education was dominated by the rigid norms of the medieval universities, as was pointed out in the case of the University of
Mexico. The Jesuits, by introducing the Greek and Roman classics
as well as realistic and humanistic studies, opened up new intellectual
vistas in Mexico. Sánchez notes the following with regard to the Colegio de San Ildefonso:

> In contrast with the narrow academic tendencies which characterized the
> Royal and Pontifical University of Mexico, San Ildefonso was a brilliant
> example of the relatively liberal curriculum sponsored by the Jesuits.
> Studies centered upon Latin grammar, philosophy, theology, canon law,
> and the humanities. The Jesuits' plan of studies and their well-ordered
> methods gave the students an education in which mild discipline, academic
> awards, public presentations, the drama and literary clubs formed an es-
> sential part of the program. Latin, Greek, Spanish and, at times, Nahuatl,
> were studied and played a part in public speeches, dramas, pageants, etc.
> Realistic studies such as physics, natural history, and mathematics had
> their place in the curriculum alongside the study of the classics.[18]

The Augustinians, the Dominicans, and the Franciscans were also
active in establishing schools and religious training centers. By the
end of the first century of Spanish colonization these three orders had
established over 300 convents among them. Probably the most pro-
lific were the Franciscans who were responsible for the founding of
over 160 convents of which there were some 145 remaining by the
end of the colonial period.[19] Two of this order's most famous schools

have already been referred to, namely, the Colegio de San José in Mexico City and the Colegio de Santa Cruz in Tlatelolco, both remarkable institutions.

The above sketch of educational foundations is not meant to cover the entire ground of colonial Spanish educational systems in Mexico. All it suggests is that Spain and the Church (one cannot be separated from the other during this period) gave all they had to the New World, at least as regards educational infrastructure, during the colonial period and particularly early in that epoch.

The Later Colonial Period

Unfortunately, the Spanish contribution later in the 17th and 18th centuries did not match the earlier effort. One reason was certainly the herculean nature of the task. There were simply not enough priests and friars to continue the job, and the Spanish government made no effort to secularize education.[20]

But there were other reasons for the decay of Mexican education late in the Spanish rule. Reference has already been made to the suppression of the Jesuits, and this dealt a blow to the institutions they founded, from which many never recovered. Moreover, the Latin American institutions, as exemplified by the University of Mexico, were committed to the scholastic Bologna-Salamanca tradition of the Southern European universities, which had been in their golden age in the 16th century. By the time New Spain was well established as a colony, however, the Southern Renaissance was in decadence, and the new leaders in world education were the Germans. Latin America was never privy to the German tradition,[21] although in the northern New World universities began to be organized after the German model during the 19th century.[22] By this time Mexico and the rest of Latin America were in the midst of picking up the pieces of some devastating revolutions. Educational infrastructure had taken a back seat to more pressing organizational problems.

The Revolutionary and Post-revolutionary Periods.

It is difficult for the uninitiated investigator to believe how politically confused Mexico was during the 19th century. Mexican independence began on September 16, 1810, when Padre Miguel Hidalgo[23] issued the famous "Cry of Dolores," and set out with his band
of tattered Indians and *mestizos* to sack the Spanish gentry and throw
them out of Mexico. Father Hidalgo apparently had no master plan;
his mob moved about from city to city, plundering as they went, setting off a race war that left untold material and psychological dam-
age. Perhaps unwilling to unleash his mob on Mexico City, Hidalgo
stopped short of an invasion of the Capitol, and the back of the in-
surrection was broken. Hidalgo and his retreating army were defeated
outside Mexico City by the pursuing Spanish troups, and again routed
near Guadalajara, despite overwhelming odds in favor of the insur-
gents. Two months later, in March 1811; Hidalgo was captured, tor-
tured, stripped of his priesthood, and shot. His head was removed
and sent to Guanajuato where it hung from a corner of the granary
for ten years as a reminder of Spanish retribution.

This was the beginning of independence[24] in Mexico, and the rest
of the tale is nearly as brutal and bewildering. Eleven years after Hidalgo's uprising and after much bloodshed, Mexico finally won her
independence in September, 1821, at the stroke of a pen. A com-
promise independence it was, since it called for Mexico to become a
constitutional monarchy under Ferdinand VII if he wished, or some
other prince of the European royal families. Agustín Iturbide, the
mestizo general who authored the independence plan,[25] assumed the
reigns of government. Iturbide spent some months going through the
motions of seeking a European prince to rule Mexico. Finally, he had
himself "acclaimed" as Emperor, and the stage was set for the long
sequence of political leaders who controlled Mexico until a second
Revolution,[26] which began in 1911, established a lasting constitutional government.

During most of this period educational development was at a vir-
tual standstill. There was, nevertheless, some school legislation. The

Constitution of 1824 had replaced Iturbide's empire with a first attempt at a Federal Republic. Following the United States' lead,[27] the republic was to be a confederation of autonomous states. In educational matters, in particular, the states were to be sovereign. The states thus worked out detailed educational plans that appeared at the time very workable on paper. Unfortunately the states lacked a financial base to support their plans, and, moreover, changes in political regimes kept rendering the plans ineffective. A school opened under one state administration might be closed by the next, and policies adopted by one executive might be rescinded by his successor.[28]

On the other hand, higher education was, according to the constitution, more in the hands of the central government. Congress was given the power to:

. . . erect establishments in which would be taught the natural and the exact sciences, . . . arts and language, without prejudicing the freedoms of the [State] legislatures in the administration of public education in their respective States.[29]

Nevertheless, in this area as well the infrastructure was awry. The University of Mexico, in full decadence by the post-revolutionary period, was suppressed in 1835, reopened and closed again several times in the middle 1800's.[30] The University of Guadalajara suffered a similar fate. Only two new universities were established, in Mérida and Chiapas, but these were, along with those of Mexico City and Guadalajara, suppressed one or more times in the 1800's.[31]

Although data are scarce, it appears that few primary schools, and even fewer secondary and higher schools were opened during the first half of the 19th century in Mexico. Of those that were open, most were private schools founded by religious orders. According to data collected by José Bravo Ugarte,[32] it appears that there were fewer than 350 primary schools in the whole Republic of Mexico in about 1850. Of these some forty percent were in Mexico City and of the total only thirty percent were public institutions. Apparently during this period there were some advances made in the private sector (mostly Church) even though the number of public schools shrank (with the exception of those of Guadalajara under the guidance of Manuel López Cotilla).

With regard to secondary schools and colleges, to the twelve existing institutions (four in the capital and eight in the provinces) 26 were added between 1827 and about 1850, of which sixteen were girls' schools opened by the Sisters of Charity. Quite obviously the opportunity for education was not being extended to the masses during this period.

In about 1858 a basic change took place in Mexican educational direction. Although still politically confused, the government of the Republic passed into the hands of Mexico's greatest patriot and one of its most honest and capable leaders of all time, Benito Juárez.[33] Juárez was a liberal, and liberalism meant in those days in Mexico, anticlericalism. A new Constitution, which came to be called La Reforma, had been written in 1857. Among other reforms this constitution called for the abolishment of church courts, dissolution of church lands, and the establishment of secular education. Only out of the hands of the Church, Juárez and the liberals believed, could mass education be insured and Mexican democracy guaranteed. As clarified in a later law, henceforth education in Mexico was to be "obligatoria, gratuita, y laica," compulsory, free, and secular. Thus the stage was set for a popular educational movement which continued into the 20th century and the tradition of which is still markedly visible today.

Nevertheless, difficult political years still lay ahead for Mexico after the bloody civil war (the War of the Reform) established liberalism in the Republic. First there was the French Intervention which lasted from 1862-1867. Juárez finally succeeded in reestablishing the Republic and then suddenly died in 1872, leaving a political vacuum that pulled into power one General Porfirio Díaz, who was to hold onto the reigns of Mexican government longer than any ruler since the Conquista.

By the time Díaz was elected, however, considerable effort at education in the spirit of the Reform had been expended. As of 1874, some 8,000 schools had been opened with a total enrollment of 350,000 children. This was hardly mass education since there were some two million children of school age in the country.[34] But the effort represented a great leap forward for Mexico in popularizing education, and set the stage for the awakening in education that swept the country in the early 20th century.

The Modern Era

Modern educational reform in Mexico dates from 1911. On May 25 of that year, Porfirio Díaz, old and sick by this time, resigned his office under great pressure. His resignation touched off another Revolution, a several year period of carnage and destruction[35] which would finally produce stable, enlightened, (and reformed) government in the Republic. By 1910, however, there were some 12,000 schools in all of Mexico and nearly 700 in the Federal District containing Mexico City. These schools had among them 25,500 teachers and were reaching nearly one million of Mexico's children, or about a fifth of the school-age population.[36] Also in 1910, the National University of Mexico was reopened after having been closed since 1865,[37] largely through the efforts of Justo Sierra, a distinguished educator who had become Minister of Public Instruction and Fine Arts under Díaz.

By 1921 Álvaro Obregón had been elected president and had succeeded in calming the political storm somewhat. A new Ministry of Public Education was established under the famous writer, philosopher, and intellectual, José Vasconcelos, and immediate attention was given to establishing schools, particularly primary schools in rural areas. Mass education in the "compulsory, free, and secular" tradition has been a major thrust of government effort ever since. By 1926, 2,600 new schools had been established in rural areas, and Vasconcelos' moto *educar es redimir* ("to educate is to redeem") was changing radically the availability of public education all over Mexico.

The 1920's and 1930's were still difficult political years in the Republic. In 1924 President Plutarco Elías Calles, a violent anti-Catholic, set forces in motion which brought about the cessation of all

Church activities in Mexico for three years (1926-1929).[38] A power-politician in the Porfirio Díaz tradition, Calles at first toyed with socialism and then ended up on the far right as a dictator with strong fascist leanings. His dominion over the Mexican political scene was brought to an end in 1936 by Mexico's first six-year president, Lázaro Cárdenas, who had been Calles' chosen candidate. Under rumors of counter-revolution, Cárdenas rounded up Calles and his cronies[39] and deported them to Los Angeles, from whence they were forbidden to return to Mexico.

During Lázaro Cárdenas' term (1934-1940), Mexico finally achieved the stable government it had so long awaited. Seven presidents have succeeded Cárdenas to date, all constitutionally and non-violently, and Mexico has passed into the modern era. The massive educational government effort has also continued apace. Literacy, which was no more than thirty percent in 1910 and fifty percent in the early 1950's, had increased by 1970 to 76 percent of the population over ten years of age.[40] By the school year 1970-71 there were nearly 50,000 primary schools and kindergartens in the country, only about eight percent of which were private. In addition, there were some 5600 secondary, preparatory, and vocational schools (57 percent private) and 125 universities (about 38 percent private). In terms of student numbers, these schools contained a total of over 9.5 million students at the primary level (again eight percent in private schools), and about 1.6 million at the middle levels, with about 29 percent of these students in private institutions. At the professional higher education level, there were a quarter of a million students, fourteen percent of whom were in private universities.[41]

In sum, in 1970 there were some 11.5 million youngsters in school in Mexico, or about 43 percent of the population between five and 29 years. On the elementary level, about 68 percent of Mexico's children were attending classes, and at the secondary level the figure was about 31 percent. University students amounted to only about three percent of their age group.[42]

In terms of expenditure on schools, Table 2-1 lists selected American countries by expenditure according to levels of public education.

Mexico has not been a leader in Latin America with regard to public expenditure on education. Only at the university level, where she ranks fourth, are Mexico's expenditures near the top of the Latin countries.

TABLE 2-1

PUBLIC RECURRING EXPENDITURE PER PUPIL ON PUBLIC EDUCATION BY LEVEL, SELECTED AMERICAN COUNTRIES, ($ U.S.)

Country	Year	Primary	Rank	Secon-dary*	Rank	3rd Level	Rank
Argentina	1969	$ 44	6	$116	8	$ 429	8
Brazil	1966	3	12	37	13	548	3
Chile	1966	56†	4	154	4	976	2
Colombia	1968	11	11	40	12	491	6
Costa Rica	1968	66	3	144	5	458	7
Ecuador	1969	32	9	158	3	231	12
Guatemala	1969	34	8	143	6	309	10
Mexico	1969	42	7	110	10	545	4
Nicaragua	1968	50	5	127	7	421	9
Panama	1969	80	2	190	2	503	5
Peru	1962	24	10	64	11	223	13
Uruguay	1965	44	6	114	9	271	11
Venezuela	1969	103	1	266	1	1903	1
Canada	1968	541‡				3183	
U.S.	1968	692‡				2044	

* includes vocational and normal training
† includes pre-primary
‡ primary and secondary

Source: UNESCO, *Statistical Yearbook, 1968*, pp. 347ff., *1970*, pp. 514ff., *1971*, pp. 548ff.

TABLE 2-2

SCHOOL ENROLLMENT BY LEVELS, SELECTED AMERICAN COUNTRIES (in thousands)

Country	Year	Total pop. 5-29 yrs.	Total enrol. all levels	(%)	5-14 yrs.	Total enrol. primary	(%)	15-19 yrs.	Total enrol. secon.	(%)	20-29 yrs.	Total enrol. univ.	(%)
Chile	1965	4376	1920	(44)	2180	1525	(70)	848	351	(41)	1348	44	(3)
Argentina	1965	9807	4167	(42)	4430	3125	(70)	1980	795	(40)	3397	247	(7)
Panama	1962	549	233	(42)	282	180	(64)	107	48	(45)	160	5	(3)
Uruguay	1963	1057	441	(42)	471	319	(68)	206	107	(52)	380	15	(4)
Costa Rica	1968	721	298	(41)	395	249	(63)	133	43	(32)	193	6	(3)
Peru	1965	6169	2472	(40)	3153	2007	(64)	1198	386	(32)	1818	79	(4)
Venezuela	1965/6	4517	1795	(40)	2371	1453	(61)	862	296	(34)	1284	46	(4)
Mexico	1965/6	23011	7970	(35)	12216	6916	(57)	4326	921	(21)	6496	133	(2)
Ecuador	1965/6	2728	933	(34)	1463	801	(55)	511	117	(23)	754	15	(2)
Colombia	1964	9418	2655	(28)	5070	2213	(44)	1766	352	(20)	2582	90	(3)
Nicaragua	1965/6	919	236	(26)	508	206	(41)	160	27	(17)	251	3	(1)
Brazil	1960*	37247	9244	(25)	18735	7835	(42)	7142	1307	(18)	11370	102	(1)
Honduras	1965	1247	311	(25)	698	284	(41)	221	24	(11)	328	3	(1)
Guatemala	1964	2244	438	(20)	1196	386	(32)	423	44	(10)	625	8	(1)
U.S.A.	1965/6	82221	54614	(66)	39474	31916	(81)	17051	17128	(100)	25696	5570	(22)
Canada	1965/6	8936	5475	(61)	4395	3566	(81)	1838	1585	(86)	2703	324	(12)

* Population 1960, enrollments 1961.

Source: United Nations, *Demographic Yearbook 1970, 1971* and UNESCO, *World Survey of Education, 1971.*

By Latin American standards, Mexico's school enrollment, too, has been rather low. Table 2-2 gives enrollments as of about 1965 in selected Latin countries. Mexico ranked eighth in this group, lower than one might expect for her leadership status among these countries. It is clear that, although she has made great progress, Mexico still faces the serious challenge of providing education for her masses of young people.

Moreover, added to this challenge is that of population growth. It took the country from 1880 to about 1940 to double its population from ten to twenty million. This figure had increased 25 percent to twenty-five million by 1950, and since 1950 the population has doubled again. Mexico is currently in the midst of a population explosion that shows little signs of abating in the very near future. A hundred million people are expected before the turn of the century, and the Republic will be hard pressed to meet the demand for education. This demand will be even more importunate at higher levels as more and more primary and secondary-trained graduates reach young adulthood, and as increased expertise and technical know-how become more necessary in a society which is growing rapidly and becoming more sophisticated. More will be said about the dimensions of this demand and its implications for the provision of higher education in Mexico in Chapter Five.

Conclusion

This chapter has undertaken a historical review of the overall educational framework in Mexico. This was done in order to understand the basic attitudes and directions that this development has taken over the years, and some of the reasons for the late development of educational infrastructure in the Republic. Mexico has finally succeeded in providing "free, compulsory, and secular" schooling to large numbers of her children, particularly at the primary level. The task remains to continue the extension of educational opportunity to even more of her young, in the face of rapid population growth. Moreover, the chance for education must be extended vertically into secondary and higher levels so that the country will have the qualified human resources so desperately needed for further growth.

REFERENCES :

1 John Edwin Fagg, *Latin America, A General History,* 1963, p. 5

2 *Ibid.,* p. 17

3 The *mestizo* mystique is an intriguing one. Possibly no subject in social literature about Mexico has received more attention. The Mexican *mestizo* is a unique combination of the fallen Indian empires and the Spanish adventurers, differing from both his parents, and the driving force in the development of his country. Apart from this mixture, Mexico remained fairly untouched by other racial inputs. For more on this concept see George Sánchez, *Mexico—A Revolution by Education,* 1936, p. 12-15.

4 George Sánchez, *The Development of Higher Education in Mexico,* 1944, p. 20.

5 *Ibid.,* p. 9. Today, Mexican official sources put the early total colonial population figure at about 7-9 million. See Secretaría de Industria y Comercio, *Anuario Estadístico de los Estados Unidos Mexicanos, 1970-71,* p. 29.

6 For their part, the "heathen Indians" were not adverse to Christianity; it was their custom anyway to accept the religion of the conquering tribe, since it was obvious that the conquerers had the stronger gods on their side. (See J. Patrick McHenry, *A Short History of Mexico,* 1970-71, p. 29).

7 To the oft-maligned Cortés is attributed the piety and foresight of having urged the sending to New Spain of clergy to teach the Indian and to begin the reconstruction of native culture. (See Paula Alegría, *La Educación en México Antes y Después de la Conquista,* 1936, p. 102, and George Sánchez, *op. cit.,* 1944, p. 31-33). It is reported that when the first large group of Franciscans (the famous Twelve) arrived in Mexico City in 1524, haggard and battered after walking all the way from Veracruz, Cortés fell to his knees and kissed the hem of their cassocks—in full view of the Indians who were astounded by the action of the great *conquistador.* (See J. P. McHenry, *op. cit.,* p. 32).

8 George Sánchez, *op. cit.,* 1944, p. 41.

9 This book follows the Mexican (and European) custom of including more than universities in the definition of an "institution of higher learning." In this case Santa Cruz was more than a primary school like the one at San José. It also offered a secondary program including logic, philosophy and science, and even a course in Indian medicine. The Mexican concept of "institution of higher learning" will be discussed further in Chapter Three.

10 G. Sánchez, *op. cit.,* 1944, p. 43.

11 José Bravo Ugarte, *La Educación en México,* 1966, p. 55.

12 A very large problem in Mexico has been and still is the preparation of teachers; there have never been enough teachers, particularly in the rural areas, and their training has never been good enough. Teachers are taught in normal schools in Mexico, not in multidisciplinary universities. Primary teachers receive only the equivalent of college preparatory training, i.e., three years after secondary.

13   Actually both were officially founded by the same decree of Charles V (Carlos I of Spain). See C. E. Castañeda, "The Beginnings of University Life in America," *Preliminary Studies of the Texas Catholic Historical Association*, July 1938, p. 7. There is also some evidence that the University of Mexico was a functioning institution as early as 1539 or 1540 and that the royal decree did but confirm an already existing reality. See J. Bravo Ugarte, *op. cit.*, p. 80-82.

14   Many authors contend that this rigid, scholastic, magisterial approach still exists in some measure in Latin universities and is the cause of a lack of emphasis on research, libraries, and independent study in the traditional universities. Other aspects of this traditionalism will be dealt with in Chapter Four.

15   G. Sánchez, *op. cit.*, 1944, p. 68.

16   C. E. Castañeda, *op. cit.*, p. 7.

17   In fact, a large element in their later (worldwide) suppression in the 1760's and 1770's was this very liberalism. For example, one author credits the Jesuits with promoting " . . . the wider diffusion of ideas which in many ways initiated heterodoxy and revolutionism." (Carlos Alvear Acevedo, *La Educación y la Ley*, 1973, p. 23). This approach to education was not at all appreciated by the Bourbon Kings of Europe.

18   G. Sánchez, *op. cit.*, 1944, p. 75.

19   G. Sánchez, *op. cit.*, 1944, p. 39; J. Bravo Ugarte, *op. cit.*, p. 53.

20   The Church would surely have opposed its doing so.

21   A main feature of this tradition was the emphasis on research in university instruction as practiced in the Universities of Berlin and Halle. A new degree reflecting a student's proficiency in research, the Ph.D., was initiated in these universities. On the contrary, the *lack* of emphasis on research in the Mexican university will be a subject of discussion in Chapter Four.

22   For an interesting summary treatment of medieval universities see Charles H. Haskins, *The Rise of Universities*, 1923. For a concise description of the German universities and their influence on U.S. institutions, see John S. Brubacher, *A History of the Problems of Education*, 1966, pp. 457-462.

23   The Father of Mexican Independence was himself an enigma. Although not particularly devout, he became a priest, probably to advance himself in the Colegio de San Nicolás in Valladolid, where he became Rector for a brief period. Soon he was in trouble with the authorities for his liberal tendencies, and was reassigned as parish priest to the humble town of Dolores, in Guanajuato. Here his unorthodoxy became well developed; he went to parties, played cards, gambled, kept mistresses, and displayed proscribed books so openly that his home became known as "Little France." Yet this same Hidalgo had a great love for the Indians of his parish and worked tirelessly at alleviating their misery and teaching them new skills. (C. E. Fagg, *op. cit.*, pp. 444-446, and J. P. McHenry, *op. cit.*, pp. 58-59.)

24   Curiously enough, Hidalgo did not mention the word "independence" when he issued his famous "cry," his call to arms in the church pulpit of Dolores. What he

advocated in that speech was the restoration of Ferdinand VII, then a prisoner of Napoleon, as rightful King of Spain. The Spanish settlers, who were all supposedly agents of Napoleon, were to be thrown out of Mexico to redress grievances.

25 Called the "Plan de Iguala", it was the first of a series of idealistic (and bombastic) pronouncements that were to characterize Mexican politics for a hundred years.

26 When Mexicans speak of their Revolution, it is this second revolution that they refer to.

27 There was one telling difference, as Alvear points out: whereas in the United States federalism served to unite the separate colonial entities, in Mexico it served to decentralize what had been united under rule of the Capitol. (Carlos Alvear A., op. cit., p. 45). This tendency to centralization will be seen again later in this book.

28 As Carlos Alvear puts, it, somewhat poetically, "The clash of political passions impeded the translation of ideas into reality." (C. Alvear A., op. cit., p. 47).

29 Article 50 of the Constitution of 1824.

30 In total the University was disestablished and re-established four times, until finally in 1910 it reopened as the National University of Mexico.

31 In addition the University of Yucatán, founded in 1644, disappeared in 1767 and was reestablished in 1824, only to close again nine years later. See Porfirio Muñoz Ledo, "La Educación Superior", in Mexico: 50 Años de Revolución, IV. La Cultura, 1960, p. 120.

32 J. Bravo U., op. cit., p. 110-121.

33 Juárez was a full-blooded Zapotec Indian, an orphaned sheepherder who had been adopted and educated by a Oaxaca family. After some years in a seminary, he elected to study law and later opened a law office for the poor in Oaxaca, where he gained a large following.

34 Data reported by J. P. McHenry, op. cit., p. 133. Also see Francisco Larroyo, Historia Comparada de la Educación en México, 1947, pp. 219-220.

35 Between 1910 and 1921 the population of the country declined by over 800,000 (or 5.4 percent) due to disease, conflict, and emigration. Secretaría de Industria y Comercio, Anuario Estadístico de los Estados Unidos Mexicanos, 1968-69, p. 29.

36 Marjorie C. Johnston, Education in Mexico, 1956, p. 24. Data cited from the Dirección General de Instrucción Primaria.

37 Final suppression had been decreed by Emperor Maximilian during the French Intervention. Apparently after the War of Independence the University degenerated steadily until it became a university in name only, conferring badly earned titles and degrees. Moreover, it was a stronghold of conservative forces and was closely aligned with the clergy. Sánchez quotes the 1940 UNAM Anuario, which gives some of the history of this period:

During those years, the conservative or reactionary governments sought to maintain [the University] for what it signified ideologically; whereas liberal and reform governments made every effort to do away with it because in no way did it corre-

spond to national educational exigencies and because it had come to be the symbol
of reactionary ideas. (G. Sánchez, *op. cit.,* 1944, p. 69).
Much to the dismay of conservative forces in Mexico at the time, Maximillian turned
out to be a liberal, and his action with regard to the University may be understood
in this light.

38 Angered by Church criticism of his government, Calles enforced the anti-
clerical laws of the Constitution of 1917 which his predecessors had ignored. In addition he had other laws passed *("la Ley Calles"):* no priest could teach in a primary
school; no priest could speak against the constitution or government; Roman collars
were prohibited. In July 1926 the Catholic Church closed its doors all over Mexico.

39 The street in Cuernavaca where Calles and his henchmen lived in gaudy
splendor was known as the "Street of the Forty Thieves." Calles had amassed great
wealth while in public office.

40 Johnston, *op. cit.,* p. 26 and Secretaría de Industria y Comercio, *Anuario Estadístico de los Estados Unidos Mexicanos, 1968-69,* p. 42.

41 Data from Secretaría de Educación Pública, *Informe de Labores, 1971,* vol. 2
pp. 17ff.; and Secretaría de Industria y Comercio, *Anuario Estadístico de los Estados
Unidos Mexicanos, 1968-69,* pp. 184ff.

42 *Ibid.* and Secretaría de Industria y Comercio *IX Censo General de Población,
1970, Resumen General Abreviado,* pp. 24ff. To calculate the elementary school population, the five to fourteen year age group was used as a base. For the secondary
population, the age group base was fifteen to nineteen years, and for the university
population, the twenty to 29 year age group. This latter group is extended to age
29 because of the widespread tendency among university students, particularly public
university students of lower income families, to attend classes part-time while they
work. This lengthens the time required to finish degrees and leads to an older student
body. See Centro de Estudios Educativos, *Diagnóstico Educativo Nacional,* 1964, p.
6, 30, 79, 100, and Charles N. Myers, *Education and National Development in Mexico,*
1965, p. 104.

III : The Dimensions and Form of Higher Education in Mexico

Although the first new world universities were established in Latin America, the Latin countries fell far behind in the eighteenth and nineteenth centuries. This is not surprising since most of the countries had post-revolutionary periods which were every bit as disruptive as Mexico's, and all were heir to the Spanish-Salamanca tradition in higher education.

By 1700, twelve universities had been founded in Latin America.[1] In the eighteenth century only six more were added, and in the entire nineteenth century, the explosive century for higher education in many parts of the world, the total number of universities in Latin America was only doubled. By the opening of the twentieth century, there were fewer than forty functioning universities in all of Latin America, only one of which was in Mexico.

This latter university was the National University of Mexico, which was reborn in 1910 with the efforts of Justo Sierra. The National University became autonomous[2] in 1929 (fully so in 1933) and is now known as the Universidad Nacional Autónoma de Mexico (UNAM). Even so, the UNAM was in 1930 little more than a loose collection of poorly attended professional schools with few professors and inadequate equipment.[3]

Outside Mexico City, in the provinces, only five of the 31 states and territories could boast of their own university by the end of the first decade after the Revolution.[4] A Polytechnic Institute was established in Mexico City as early as 1922, but in its initial form its curricula were by and large limited to middle-level and technical education.[5] By 1940, there were a total of only nine universities in Mexico, of which the Autonomous University of Guadalajara was the singular private institution.[6]

Since 1940 there has been a takeoff in higher education in the Republic, and Mexico has moved forward rapidly in both public and private sectors. By 1971, 125 universities were in operation in the country, 77 of which were public (62 percent) and 48 private.[7]

Before going on, it will be useful to understand more fully what a university consists of in Mexico. Only a general outline will be presented here. For a more complete descriptive treatment, see, for example, Marjorie Johnston's *Education in Mexico* or Clark Gill's *Education in a Changing Mexico.*

In Mexico and Latin America education is by professional school, or *carrera*, literally "career," but roughly translatable under the American concept of a "major" subject. However, the Latin concept is quite different from that of the United States because the Latin American student begins to specialize in his major from the very first semester. This arrangement will be familiar to students who have gone to school in the European tradition, but in the Latin American context the "career" takes on some special characteristics of educational isolationism about which more will be said in Chapter Four. For the present it is to be noted that the Latin student chooses his career before entry to the university, and he matriculates in the professional school which offers him a "permit" to practice that profession.

Most *carreras* are for a duration of five years. This means that by graduation most Mexican students have been specializing in their field for ten semesters. Therefore, although they have little contact with other disciplines, they have had as much training in their own field as most master's degree students in the United States, depending upon the quality of their university's program.

The most popular careers in Latin America have been philosophy and humanities, followed by law and social sciences, and by medicine and dentistry.[8] In Mexico the focus is more practical and scientific, reflecting the pragmatic kind of development model that characterizes the country. Engineering draws the most students, 67,000 in 1971, followed by business administration and accounting (55,000), and then medicine and dentistry (45,000).[9] By his completion of a given *carrera* at a professional school, the student receives his "license" or *licenciatura* to practice his chosen profession.

Another difference in the Mexican approach to higher education is that the *preparatoria*, or preparatory school, is frequently a part of the university itself. This is probably partly a result of the tradition of the early Mexican *colegios,* and partly a continuation of the Salamanca tradition.[10] In any case, 56 or forty-five percent of the 125 Mexican universities have *"prepas"* (not counting the nineteen higher-normal schools which are specialization schools for primary teachers). Thus, in these pages an "institution of higher learning" in Mexico will include the preparatory school so typically an integral part of the university.[11] Where possible, data on university enrollment, etc. will be specified as to the inclusion of the *prepas* and other dependencies.

The pattern of education in Mexico is translatable into the U.S. 6/3/3 plan of elementary/junior high/high school. Six years of elementary school *(primaria)* are followed by three years *secundaria* which are followed by two to three[12] more years of *preparatoria.* Upon attaining the *bachillerato* from the *prepa,* the student is eligible for the university professional school. There is somewhat more program flexibility than this, since many schools (about 65 in 1971) operate what are called *medio profesional* (sub-professional) programs. After *secundaria,* the student may go into a two-to-three-year technical program to become, for example, a nurse, laboratory technician, electrical technician, etc. There is some indication that these shorter programs are becoming more popular among Mexican young people, but by far and away the most popular pathway is the traditional *prepa-*professional school in which the students outnumbered those of the technical schools by twelve to one in 1971.

Private and Public Universities

In 1970-71 there were about 257,000 students registered in the professional schools of all the 125 universities of Mexico.[13] There were over 186,000 more in the university preparatory schools, and the number of graduate students in all the universities of the Republic amounted to about 6,500. Enrollment distribution between public and private institutions can be seen in Table 3-1.

Even though private institutions of higher learning amount to some 38 percent of the total number of institutions, they contain less than twelve percent of the total students. The importance of the public institutions is even greater at the *prepa* level where only 7.4 percent of the students attend private universities.[14] At the level of the largest number of students, in the professional schools, only about fourteen percent of the registered students are in private institutions.

Thus the public universities dominate higher education in Mexico as they do in several other countries in Latin America, notably Argentina and Venezuela, in Central America, and in most European countries. The public-private mix that is characteristic of the U.S. and particularly of Japan (where there are many more private university students than public) did not occur in Mexico.[15]

Looking closer at the enrollment data for Mexican universities, the most obvious implication would be that public institutions are much larger than private ones. This is true, but in a rather special way. Table 3-2 lists the ten largest universities, in 1967-68 and 1970-71.

All of the institutions in Table 3-2 are public except two, the Monterrey Technological Institute (Instituto Tecnológico y de Estudios Superiores de Monterrey — ITESM) and the Autonomous University of Guadalajara (Universidad Autónoma de Guadalajara — UAG).

TABLE 3-1

ENROLLMENT, MEXICAN PUBLIC AND PRIVATE UNIVERSITIES, 1970-71

	Total	%	Prepas	%	Professional Schools	%	Graduate Schools	%
Public Universities	398,297	88.6	172,435	92.6	220,324	85.8	5538	85.7
Private Universities	51,167	11.4	13,816	7.4	36,428	14.2	923	14.3
	449,464	100.0	186,251	100.0	256,752	100.0	6461	100.0

Source: Asociación Nacional de Universidades e Institutos de Enseñanza Superior, *La Enseñanza Superior en México*, 1971, pp. 29ff.

TABLE 3-2

ENROLLMENTS* LARGEST MEXICAN UNIVERSITIES
1967-68 and 1970-71

Institution	1967-68	Rank	1970-71	Rank
National University of Mexico	89,799	1	134,937	1
National Polytechnic Institute	54,057	2	81,026	2
University of Guadalajara	21,597	3	31,602	3
University of Veracruz	13,759	4	9,248†	7
University of Nuevo León	13,620	5	20,622	4
Autonomous University of Puebla	9,496	6	12,873	5
Monterrey Technological Institute	6,265	7	6,599	10
University of Michoacán	6,056	8	9,483	6
Autonomous University of San Luis Potosí	5,823	9	8,799	8
Autonomous University of Guadalajara	4,627	10	8,328	9

* Includes graduate, professional, and preparatory schools.

† In 1968-69, the University of Veracruz *prepas* and secondary schools were separated from the University. Hence enrollments "fell."

Source: ANUIES, *La Enseñanza Superior en México, 1968,* pp. 19ff., *1971,* pp. 29ff.

The picture of public-private higher education thus emerges. Mexican universities are dominated by a few very large institutions, principally public ones, two of which alone (the National University and National Polytechnic) absorb nearly fifty percent of all students in the Republic. The two behemoths happen to be located in Mexico City, about which more will be said in the next section of this chapter. The remaining universities, both public and private, are of a middling or small size; 82 of the 125 universities in 1970-71 had less than 1,000 students in their graduate, professional and preparatory schools and only 25 had enrollments over 3,000. Out of these 25, only five are private, so that the bulk of public universities tends to be larger than the private institutions.

Capitol and Provincial Differences

Another important fact of life in Mexico is the centralization of activity in a few geographically small population centers, principally Mexico City.[16]

Since pre-Hispanic times, Mexico City has had domain over its environs. It was in Mexico City and the surrounding high plateau ("*altiplano*") that the Spanish found the most advanced cultures, the gold and silver mines, and the most agreeable climate. Later the centralist character of the Spanish colonial government gave primacy to the capitol city as a political center, and as population grew, Mexico City became the only market of importance in the country. Thus it has happened that the center of Mexican politics, industry, and commerce have all come to rest in Mexico City, and it is there that Mexican development has reached its full florescence.

There are a few other population centers of secondary importance. Guadalajara, an old city of the *altiplano* (founded in 1529) has become a fast-growing metropolis since the 1950's, and is Mexico's second city. Monterrey, a city which is itself the product of industrial growth since about 1900, is the third largest Mexican metropolitan area.[17] There are a handful of other population centers experiencing rapid growth and increasing wealth, such as Ciudad Juárez, Chihuahua, and Tijuana, Baja California. But there remain broad expanses of Mexican countryside, particularly in the south, which have been relatively untouched by the economic development that has characterized Mexico in the post-World-War-II period.

Educational infrastructure is fairly unevenly distributed as well. Contrasting the Federal District and some of the more advanced northern and western states with some of the poorer central and southern states, the results resemble those of Table 3-3, with respect to educational indices like self-reported literacy and school attendance.

Although literacy rates are significantly different between the Federal District and the more advanced and less advanced areas, it is noteworthy that the school attendance rates are not so different.

As was pointed out in Chapter 2, Mexico has been putting considerable emphasis on mass education, and literacy rates are rising all over the country.

Students and facilities in higher education would be expected to be distributed similarly. Table 3-4 shows the concentration of universities and their students (including *prepas*) which existed in the Federal District in 1970-71.

More than half of all Mexico's students were going to school in Mexico City. The number of institutions in the capital is less striking, but of course this figure is virtually meaningless except in terms of choice for the student.

TABLE 3-3

LITERACY AND SCHOOL ATTENDANCE, SELECTED MEXICAN STATES
1970

	% literacy, population 10 yrs. and older 1970	*% population (1970) 6-29 yrs. old attending school*
More advanced areas:		
Federal District	90.0	50.9
Nuevo León (contains Monterrey)	89.3	47.6
Baja California	88.2	45.4
Coahuila	87.6	42.8
Chihuahua	87.1	43.0
Sonora	86.4	43.0
Jalisco (contains Guadalajara)	80.6	41.9
Less advanced areas:		
Guanajuato	64.7	32.0
Hidalgo	62.1	37.9
Querétaro	62.1	36.7
Oaxaca	57.8	38.2
Chiapas	56.7	28.4
Guerrero	55.4	37.4

Source: Secretaría de Industria y Comercio, *Anuario Estadístico Compendiado, 1970*, p. 28, and Secretaría de Industria y Comercio, *IX Censo General de Población, 1970, Resumen General Abreviado*, pp. 89ff.

The reason for this concentration of students is not at all surprising at this point since it will be remembered that the UNAM and the National Polytecnic Institute (Instituto Politécnico Nacional — IPN) contain nearly half of Mexico's professional school students. If graduate and preparatory schools are included,[18] the UNAM in 1971 had a total of some 135,000 students (not counting some 3,500 more in secondary and *medio profesional* schools which are a part of the UNAM complex.)[19] The numbers with respect to the IPN are less startling, but nevertheless impressive: in 1970-71 the total student body (as previously defined) was over 80,000.

Thus, these two mammoth institutions alone absorb 88 percent of Mexico City's university students. The remaining twelve percent, or about 28.8 thousand students are distributed among the other 34 universities, the very largest of which contained only 5,000 students and is a private institution (Iberoamerican University).

The implications of the above figures are striking indeed because they indicate centralization within centralization. In Mexico City students have a wide choice of universities, some 36 to choose from.[20] Yet nearly 90 percent select the big federal universities, which are filled to overcrowding.[21] And this overcrowding has some implications for quality, as will be seen in Chapter Four.

TABLE 3-4

DISTRIBUTION OF STUDENTS AND UNIVERSITIES, FEDERAL DISTRICT AND ELSEWHERE, 1970-71

	No. universities	%	No. students	%
Federal District	36	28.9	244,715	54.4
Elsewhere	89	71.1	204,749	45.6
	125	100.0	449,464	100.0

Source: ANUIES, *La Enseñanza Superior en México, 1971*, pp. 29ff.

State and Regional Differences

Looking at the Mexican states with respect to university enrollment, a picture of student distribution emerges very much like that
of Table 3-2 earlier. Table 3-5 ranks the top ten states with regard
to student enrollment, *prepas* and above.

TABLE 3-5

UNIVERSITY ENROLLMENTS, TEN LEADING STATES, 1970-71

		Total enrollment	State per-capita product 1970 ($US)
1.	Federal District	244,715	$1657
2.	Jalisco	41,148	538
3.	Nuevo León	34,740	1220
4.	Puebla	12,873	388
5.	Veracruz	10,637	524
6.	Michoacán	9,821	321
7.	San Luis Potosí	8,961	490
8.	Coahuila	8,285	1135
9.	State of México	7,903	601
10.	Chihuahua	6,350	648

Source: Same as Table 3-4 for enrollments. Product data from Organización de Na-
ciones Unidas, Proyecto de Desarrollo Regional y Urbano de México, "Pro-
ducto Geográfico Bruto a Precios Corrientes de las Entidades Federativas,
1960, 1965, 1970," unpublished.

Comparing Table 3-5 with 3-2, the same states appear, represent-
ing the large universities they contain. Jalisco and Nuevo León each
have two large institutions, one public (University of Guadalajara
and University of Nuevo León) and the other private (Autonomous
University of Guadalajara and Monterrey Technological Institute).
The other states each have one larger, established university in their
capitol cities. The last three states are new entries to the group of
states included in Table 3-2. Two of these are wealthier states along
the northern border, Coahuila and Chihuahua, and the third, the

State of México, includes a growing industrial and suburban area around the capitol.[22]

Table 3-5 also presents U.N. data on per-capita product of the enrollment leaders since it might be thought that university inscriptions are an indicator of the wealth of a state. It is reasonable to assume that in Mexico as elsewhere, higher education is an income-elastic good. Indeed, this is the kind of hypothesis forwarded by Paul Yates and Charles N. Myers who point to the differences in educational infrastructure between the richer capitol and northern areas and the poorer southern and central areas, a dichotomy briefly reviewed in the last section.[23, 24]

Among all states in the Republic, median product is approximately $500 U.S., and so all but two states in Table 3-5, Puebla and Michoacán, are near or above the average. However, a rank correlation by state between per-capita product and per-capita university enrollment yields a low correlation coefficient, indicating that less than fifteen percent of the variance in enrollment by state is associated with differences in income levels.[25] Thus it would appear that state wealth is not a good predictor of university enrollment.

Further, Table 3-6 presents university enrollment by regions, using the ANUIES classification, and compares regions by percent of college-age population enrolled.[26] As noted earlier, the Federal District is far and away the nation's largest educator at the university level, compared to other regions, even the wealthier northern areas.

What the above analyses suggest is that, rather than an income-related or regional phenomenon, university enrollment is an urban phenomenon, particularly as the regards the primary urban area, the Federal District. In every single case among the states in Table 3-5, their principal universities are located in the state's principal (and capitol) city. Outside of these cities there is little university activity carried on. Thus, the centralization characterized in the last section has a further dimension: universities in Mexico are urban entities, serving the capitol cities of their states. These cities tend to be in the wealthier areas of the country, but also exist in other established cities such as Morelia (Michoacán), Puebla, and San Luis Potosí.

TABLE 3-6

UNIVERSITY ENROLLMENT BY REGIONS, 1970-71

		Enrollment	As percent of 1970 population aged 15-29
I	NORTHWEST (Baja California Norte, Chihuahua, Sinaloa, Sonora)	22,525	1.8
II	NORTH (Coahuila, Nuevo León, Tamaulipas)	48,264	4.4
III	CENTRAL (Aguascalientes, Durango, Querétaro, San Luis Potosí, Zacatecas)	17,056	1.5
IV	WEST (Colima, Guanajuato, Jalisco, Michoacán, Nayarit)	61,785	2.9
V	SOUTH CENTRAL (Guerrero, Hidalgo, México, Morelos, Puebla, Tlaxcala)	31,799	1.3
VI	SOUTH (Chiapas, Oaxaca, Tabasco, Veracruz)	18,602	0.9
VII	SOUTHEAST (Campeche, Yucatán)	4,718	1.8
	DISTRITO FEDERAL	244,715	12.3

Source: ANUIES, *La Enseñanza Superior en México, 1971,* pp. 29ff.

The reasons for this phenomenon may be thought to be part of the general centralist tendencies left by the colonial tradition, and the fact that development has taken place around these poles. However, a further explanation[27] may lie in the fact that the cities in a region, particularly wealthier, capitol cities, are absorbers of underemployment in the countryside. With a surplus labor supply in the cities, employment opportunities are increasingly based on educational attainment. Thus school enrollment pressures are particularly heavy in the cities, especially at higher levels where education is not elsewhere obtainable.

Student Profile

This section presents a profile of all students by sex, by distribution in *prepa* and professional school, and by level of attainment.

Table 3-7 gives the same enrollment information as Table 3-1, but broken down by sex. It will be no surprise that Mexico, a male oriented society, has about eighty percent male enrollment at all university levels. This proportion has changed somewhat during the past few years, as can be seen comparing Tables 3-7 and 3-8, with women's enrollment increasing by three percentage points during the last decade.

TABLE 3-7

ENROLLMENT BY SEX, MEXICAN UNIVERSITIES, 1970-71

	Total	%	Prepas	%	Professional Schools	%	Graduate Schools	%
Men	356,636	79.4	146,292	78.6	204,918	79.8	5426	84.0
Women	92,828	20.6	39,959	21.4	51,834	20.2	1035	16.0
Totals	449,464	100.0	186,251	100.0	256,752	100.0	6461	100.0

Source: ANUIES, *La Enseñanza Superior en México, 1971*, pp. 59ff.

TABLE 3-8

PERCENT ENROLLMENT BY SEX
[*PREPAS* AND PROFESSIONAL SCHOOLS ONLY]
1961 AND 1965

	1961	1965
Men	82.4	81.4
Women	17.6	18.6
	100.0	100.0

Source: Secretaría de Industria y Comercio, *Anuario Estadístico de los Estados Unidos Mexicanos, 1962-63* and *1966-67, passim.* ("*Educación y Cultura*" Section.)

Although it might be suspected that all Latin American universities would be male-dominated institutions, Mexico's enrollment of women in universities in sharp contrast to that of some other Latin countries where higher female enrollment ratios exist. For example, in Chile enrollment of women in university careers was as high as 31 percent in 1965. In Argentina, Costa Rica, and Uruguay the figure was nearly thirty percent in 1968-69. Several other countries in Latin America reported percentages of female enrollment higher than 25 percent in the late 1960's[28] In general, then, Mexico's inclusion of women in university study has been low by Latin American standards, and it would appear that the country has not yet begun to include its women in professional life alongside their male counterparts.

With regard to the distribution of students by year in *prepa* and professional schools, Table 3-9 shows the detail for 1967-68.[29] The pyramid of progression is well formed, with four times as many students in the first year of *prepa* as in the last years of professional school, reflecting not only the dropout rate, but also the tremendous growth that higher education is experiencing under the post-1950 population explosion.

TABLE 3-9

ENROLLMENTS OF PREPARATORY AND PROFESSIONAL SCHOOLS,
BY YEAR LEVEL, 1967-68

			Total No. of students by year, 1967-68	%
Preparatorias	1		74,543	51.1
	2		57,648	39.5
	3		13,606*	9.4
		Total	145,797	100.0
Professional Schools	1		55,487	32.8
	2		38,906	23.0
	3		30,242	17.9
	4		25,866	15.3
	5 or higher		18,501	11.0
		Total	169,002	100.0

* See text.

Source: ANUIES, *La Enseñanza Superior en México,* 1968, pp. 61ff, pp. 131ff.

A few comments are in order concerning Table 3-9. First as mentioned earlier in this chapter, the National University changed its preparatory school curriculum from a two to three year program; 10,600 of the students in the third year of *prepa* were at the UNAM.

Secondly, most *carreras* in Mexico have been for a period of five years, as already explained. Included in the fifth-year figures of Table 3-9, however, are some 2400 sixth-year students, almost all of which are medical students doing their year of social service after internship.[30] Some other careers are of four years duration, notably higher normal school training (which is specialization in a discipline) and a few other fields at some universities. It might be mentioned that there is some pressure in other careers to shorten the time to graduation to four years. For example, many *carreras* at the UNAM now consist of eight or nine semesters of course work.

The concept of "graduation" from a professional school should be clarified since it is different from that of the United States. When a student completes his course work at the end of five (or four) years, he receives a *"carta de pasante,"* a letter of completion. This is not really the "license" to practice his profession, or *"licenciatura,"* which is formally received only after completion of the *"tesis profesional"* or undergraduate thesis. Only upon termination and defense of the thesis is the *"título profesional"* granted, which is formal recognition of the student's professional standing.

But neither all nor nearly all of the *pasantes*[31] become full-fledged professionals, and thereby hangs a problem. The professional thesis represents the student's first really independent effort in his field. Term papers are not a part of the course curricula in most universities, even less so in the *prepas.* So the student arrives at his final year of college having survived his coursework but essentially having done no research of his own. Two conclusions follow: first, the professional thesis tends to be pedestrian, or bombastic, or frequently little more than a matter of pure form. Secondly, many theses simply are not completed, and the new professional enters his field without a full-fledged *licenciatura.*[32] Since not all employers demand the *título profesional* as a precondition for employment, and since many young graduates go to work for family (or friends' family)[33] firms, the thesis is frequently forgotten.

It is difficult to measure accurately how many *pasantes* finish their theses. In 1970-71 there were about 26,000 *egresados*, or graduates-*pasantes*, of the professional schools of Mexico, and about 14,000 *titulados*. Since most students who do finish theses do so in the first year or two after graduation, the number of *titulados* in any given year will serve as a conservative approximation of the correct figure of those who finished from the previous year's group. Yearly comparisons are given in Table 3-10. Thus it might be fair to say that fifty to sixty percent of Mexican professionals in the late 1960's became "fully qualified" members of their profession.

TABLE 3-10

EGRESADOS AND *TITULADOS*, PROFESSIONAL SCHOOLS,
1967-68 to 1970-71

Year	Egresados	Titulados	Titulados (year) ÷ Egresados (year-1)
1967-68	16,483	9,017	----
1968-69	20,797	10,058	61%
1969-70	22,904	11,264	49
1970-71	25,793	13,749	60

Source: ANUIES, *La Enseñanza Superior en México, 1968,* p. 319, *1969,* p. 146, *1970,* p. 21, *1971,* p. 17-18.

The final measure of attainment levels that will be attempted here will be the university dropout rate. Table 3-11 gives the total enrollment at the beginning of courses during several years, and the aggregated dropouts in all grade levels and careers during the year. No clear-cut patterns emerge from Table 3-11 except that the overall dropout rate per year in both *prepas* and professional schools is only about five percent on an average. This seems to indicate that desertion from the university is relatively low overall; students fortunate enough to enter the university tend to stay there and to complete their careers (whether or not they also finish their theses).

TABLE 3-11

UNIVERSITY ENROLLMENTS AND DROPOUTS, 1960's

Year		PREPARATORY SCHOOLS			PROFESSIONAL SCHOOLS		
		Inscriptions	Drops	%	Inscriptions	Drops	%
1961	men	41,065	2,214	5.4	68,563	2,415	3.5
	women	8,960	429	4.8	14,502	646	4.4
1963	men	53,568	3,377	6.3	85,214	3,589	4.2
	women	12,145	667	5.5	19,504	1,406	7.2
1965	men	59,628	4,701	7.9	108,235	4,855	4.5
	women	15,738	1,154	7.3	22,613	903	4.0
1967	men	86,825	5,234	6.0	113,143	5,404	4.8
	women	24,474	1,247	5.1	21,908	779	3.6
1969	men	101,461	5,335	5.2	142,215	6,324	4.4
	women	32,565	1,504	4.6	31,544	1,247	3.9

Table note: The resulting figure of substracting drops from inscriptions would be the enrollment at the end of courses.

Source: Secretaría de Industria y Comercio, *Anuario Estadístico de los Estados Unidos Mexicanos, 1962-63, 1964-65, 1968-69* and *1970-71*, Tables 6-28 and 6-29, all editions.

TABLE 3-12

PROFESSIONAL SCHOOL TRAINING AMONG PERSONS
TWENTY YEARS AND OLDER
1970

Total population 20 years and older, 1970	20,884,167
Total with some professional school training	537,789
1 year finished	87,702
2 years finished	77,822
3 years finished	75,406
4 years finished	78,081
5 years finished	218,778

Source: Secretaría de Industria y Comercio, *IX Censo General de Población, 1970, Resumen General Abreviado*, p. 97.

This conclusion is borne out by data from the 1970 census. Of those persons who confessed to census takers in 1970 some college experience, fully forty percent had finished five years of college training. Of the total Mexican population twenty years and older, the distribution of years finished was as indicated in Table 3-12.

In Table 3-12, the largest group by far are persons who have completed five years of college and are presumably at least *pasantes*. Considering there are some four-year careers, particularly for school teachers, those persons who have completed course work for their degree probably amount to over half of the college-trained Mexicans.

Returning to Table 3-11, it appears that men drop at a slightly higher rate than women. Although one might expect women to drop out at a higher rate than men due to marriage and other considerations, this does not seem to be true in the years considered. In all years at the *prepa* level and in three of the five years at the university level, men dropped out more than did women. This may reflect a relatively higher opportunity cost for men to attend school at these levels. In a well-known article on rates of return to education, Martin Carnoy found that the opportunity cost of not working (i.e. earnings foregone) for urban males exceeds public and private institutional costs as early as the fourth year of primary school and represents " . . . about sixty percent of total expenditures on schooling from the fifth or sixth grade of primary school through university."[34] It would appear that men respond to these high opportunity costs by dropping out of *prepas* and professional schools at a higher rate than women.

Of course, dropout rates will vary over careers and over year levels and particularly as between institutions. One study which has been attempted in this area was done with regard to the 26 medical schools (as of 1971) in the country.[35] According to this study, the dropout rates in these schools vary from about twenty percent over a five-year period (that is, eighty percent of students entering in first year leave as *pasantes* after five years) up to about 70-75 percent. The smallest drop rates appear to be among the larger, more prestigious institutions. Some of the drops are transfers to other schools, and a phenomenon which seems to show up here is the transfer from smaller, outlying schools to the larger schools in important metropolitan areas. For example, the UNAM medical school (which contained over 16,000 students in 1970-71) showed up in this study to have a drop rate across the five years from 1966 to 1971 of only about one percent. Virtually as many students finished their careers as had begun them five years earlier. The explanation here lies in the large number of transfers from the provincial universities to the giant university of the capitol, a process of centralization which has been seen before in this chapter.

A fact worth mentioning here is the apparent lack of transfers *between* careers. Because of the immediate specialization of the students and the general lack of core courses that all students take (more about this in Chapter Four), students who change their minds about their career choice must start all over again in another professional school, with no credit for work already done. This naturally limits career changes to those students who have failed in their first choice and have nothing to lose by transferring.

Conclusion

This chapter has been an attempt to describe some of the salient features of the structure of higher education in Mexico. The picture emerges of a European-style system of higher instruction which developed very late in Mexican history; about 1940 counts as the takeoff date for Mexican higher education. Much has been done in the thirty-odd years since that date. Mexican higher education, it is seen, is far more public than private and the university is a microcosm of the socety in that it reflects the centralization of economic life around a few metropolitan poles, especially Mexico City. In particular, statistics on total university enrollment conceal the fact that half of that enrollment is contained in two duolithic federal institutions in Mexico City. The rest is distributed among much smaller institutions in Mexico City and other large cities of the provinces.

Finally, university students in Mexico are predominately male, but enrollments of both sexes are increasing rapidly. Students who are able to attend college tend to finish the career that they have begun, even though they may not do the thesis required for full professional status; independent study and research are not yet an integral part of university life.

Having made this general sketch of all Mexican universities, the following chapters present a further analysis of the institutions and their development, focusing on the relationship between the universities and Mexico's educational needs.

REFERENCES:

1 The data in this paragraph are quoted from Richard G. King, *The Provincial Universities of Mexico,* 1971, p. 6.

2 "Autonomy" is an important concept in Mexican higher education, but a hard one to define. Generally it refers to freedom from governmental economic and political intervention, a movement which began at the University of Córdoba, Argentina, in 1918. But some of both private and public universities in Mexico carry "autonomous" as part of their names. The meaning of the concept will become clearer in the next chapter.

3 Charles Nash Myers, *Education and National Development in Mexico,* 1965, p. 100.

4 J. Bravo Ugarte, *La Educación en México,* 1966, p. 178.

5 This early Institute was actually a group of some 17 technical and commercial schools which were organized under a Federal Department of Technical, Industrial, and Commercial Instruction in 1923. The National Polytechnic Institute was officially founded in 1937 by President Lázaro Cárdenas.

6 The Universidad Obrera de México is also listed by George Sánchez *(The Development of Higher Education in Mexico,* 1944, p. 98) and categorized as a private institution by J. Bravo U., *op. cit.,* p. 180. Since it was a socialist institution offering part-time, non-degree continuation courses to workers, and since it was under the supervision of the Labor Department of the Government, it is not included in the nine institutions mentioned in the text. For further information on this period of educational development, also see Porfirio Muñoz Ledo, "La Educación Superior," in *México: 50 Años de Revolución IV. La Cultura,* 1960, pp. 120ff.

7 This chapter draws substantially on data from the Asociación Nacional de Universidades e Institutos de Enseñanza Superior (ANUIES), *La Enseñanza Superior en México, 1971,* published in June, 1974.

8   Richard G. King, *op. cit.*, p. 9. Data from Social Progress Trust Fund (1967).

9   ANUIES, *op. cit.* (1971), p. 244.

10   In the medieval universities the bachelors' degree was merely a permission to become a candidate for an advanced degree. The student usually spent the first year at the university perfecting his Latin (university courses were conducted, of course, in Latin), while he was beginning to study the arts. After this training, he was admitted to the degree bachelor of arts, and to candidacy for the coveted degree master of arts, which was the "license" to teach or practice the profession. (See John S. Brubacher, *A History of the Problems of Education*, 1966, p. 429ff.) Similarly in Mexico, the student receives his *bachillerato* after two to three years of preparatory study and his *licenciatura* after completing his professional specialization.

11   In addition, fifteen of the universities which have *prepas* also have secondary schools.

12   The standard length of the *prepa* cycle is two years. However, in 1964 the National University extended the cycle from two to three years for itself and its dependent institutions (and lowered the class hours each year) in order to reduce enrollment pressure on itself.

13   ANUIES, *op. cit.*, p. 16.

14   The reason for the larger number of public *prepa* students stems from the fact that the largest of the large public universities also have large *prepas*. The *prepas* tend to be smaller in the private institutions. In addition, it appears that there has been, in recent years, an overall shift toward more public preparatory education among students. Between 1964 and 1970, public preparatory enrollment rose 110 percent while private enrollment rose 80 percent. (These figures include *all prepas*, not only those which are run by universities. This growth will be commented upon further in the next chapter.) In these same years, 1964 and 1970, public professional schools have grown 67 percent while private schools have increased their student bodies by 61 percent. (See Secretaría de Educación Pública, *La Educación Pública en México, 1964-1970*, Vol. 2 pp. 302ff.)

15   For complete school enrollment data country by country, in 1965-66, see UNESCO, *World Survey of Education*, 1971.

16   Technically, the capitol city is bounded geographically by a special government "Department" called the Federal District. But actually the "city" includes many outside suburbs (the metropolitan complex is generally called the Valley of Mexico) much like the Washington, D.C. metropolitan area. However, Mexico City dominates national life considerably more than does Washington (Mexico City is known simply as "Mexico," such is its importance!), and the District of Columbia would have to contain some 30 million people in order to match "Mexico's" importance in terms of population.

17   For comparison, the population of Mexico City (Federal District only) in 1970 was 6.9 million; Guadalajara 1.2 million; Monterrey 830 thousand.

18   The breakdown for UNAM is as follows for 1970-71:

Graduate schools	3,819
Professional schools	73,792
Prepas	57,326
Total	134,937

19   By 1974-75 this figure had risen to nearly 260,000!

20   This is not exactly accurate since three of the universities are military academies and one is exclusively a graduate school.

21   New rules since about 1966 attempt to limit enrollment of provincial students in the UNAM and the National Polytechnic.

22   The State of Mexico nearly encloses the Federal District and since about 1963 has been responsible for an increasing measure of the industrial activity of the country.

23   Paul Lamartine Yates, *El Desarrollo Regional de México,* 1965, pp. 88ff. Yates uses the level of educational services as an indicator of welfare, relating it to income/ production per capita by state. He indicates that the richest states are also the most favored on a broad measure of welfare, including education.

24   Charles Nash Myers, *op. cit.,* pp. 142ff., further contends that the Republic has acted correctly in allocating more educational investment to the advanced areas where return to the investment would be greater.

25   $r^2 = .1262$. Population aged 15-29 used as a base for comparison with total university enrollment.

26   This classification is different from that used by the General Statistics Office, which is based on agricultural production zones.

27   I am indebted to Michael Todaro of the Rockefeller Foundation for this point.

28   UNESCO, *Statistical Yearbook, 1971,* pp. 369ff.

29   1968-69 is the last year that ANUIES compiled enrollment data by year level for the Mexican universities. Because of anomalies in the 1968-69 figures, data from 1967-68 are used here.

30   The medical student in Mexico and elsewhere in Latin America is like any other professional student in that he begins medical study immediately after preparatory school. In most universities the student spends four years in theoretical and clinical study, and a fifth year as an intern. There is no pre-medical program as such.

31   A *pasante* is one who has passed all his courses and received his *carta de pasante* but has not completed his thesis.

32   This situation is complicated by the fact that a *pasante* will be addressed as "*Licenciado*" even though he doesn't have his thesis completed. This question follows through to the doctoral level, so that a doctoral candidate with his thesis pending may be called "doctor." This reflects further the general underemphasis on research as an integral part of degree work.

33 The *"compadrazgo"* system is well-developed in Mexico. This refers to the custom of interlocking families by serving as godfather for a close friend's children. Thus one becomes a *compadre* of the friend. The *compadre* relationship goes much deeper than that of simple spiritual parenthood, however, and implies broad business and social obligations between individuals. For some of the flavor of this social institution, see, for example, Marco Almazán, *El Rediezcubrimiento de México,* 1970, Ch. 6.

34 Martin Carnoy, "Rates of Return to Schooling in Latin America," *Journal of Human Resources,* Summer 1967, p. 362.

35 Centro de Investigaciones Económicas y de Negocios, Universidad Autónoma de Guadalajara, *Reporte Dos: Médicos en México, Preliminar,* 1971.

IV : MEXICAN PUBLIC AND PRIVATE UNIVERSITIES —
GROWTH AND QUALITY CONSIDERATIONS

UP TO THIS POINT, the ANUIES[1] definition of "public" and "private" universities has been implicitly accepted since this has been the source for measures of variables among universities. Before going on, the distinction between public and private institutions in Mexico should be made clearer.

In the ANUIES data, and in common usage in Mexico, the public, or "official," universities are those that were formed by decree of the Federal or State governments under powers of the Constitution. Only these universities, under the concept of secular education contained in the Constitutions of 1857 and 1917, have the power to grant degrees, thus "licensing" persons to practice a profession in Mexico. The public university may be "autonomous" like the National University of Mexico, which selects its own Rector (president) and whose Board of Governors are formed entirely of officials within the university, and students.[2] Of course the government (Federal as in the case of the UNAM, the National Polytechnic Institute and a few others) is responsible for the total funding of the universities, except for minimal tuition charges and donations.[3] Or the public university may lack titular autonomy, in which case the government, usually the state government, participates in some way in the internal governing process of the university. For example, at the University of Guadalajara, the state governor picks the Rector from a slate of three candidates given him by the University Council.[4] Otherwise, state officials do not ordinarily interfere in university functions even though the relationship between government and university officials may be a close one. Even in the non-autonomous universities, political appointments of professors or administrators are rare, and universities no longer change hands with changing political administrations as they did in the post-colonial period.

The private universities, on the other hand, while they are virtually totally independent financially[5] and ordinarily receive no government appropriation, must conform to curriculum standards established by the UNAM or the National Polytechnic, a state university or government, or the Secretaría de Educación Pública (or another secretariat, as in the case of the military academies). Again, only government has the constitutional power to grant degrees in Mexico, so the typical private university, like the Autonomous University of Guadalajara, must have its studies "incorporated" into those of the UNAM, for which privilege it pays a fee. Thereby the degrees granted at the UAG are UNAM degrees and have legal validity.

A very few Mexican private universities have been able to establish complete autonomy, both financial and curricular. These are the so-called *"universidades libres"* ("free universities") which have been given degree-granting powers by government (presidential) decree. Apparently there are both quality and political considerations involved in attaining *universidad libre* status, and this status does not seem to determine the prestige of the institution. In 1970-71, there were seven of these free universities, the largest of which was Monterrey Technological Institute.[6]

In the ANUIES data there is only one university that is a true mixture of public and private sectors, *El Colegio de México* in Mexico City. This institution is unique in more than one way since it is very small, yet highly reputed, and is mainly a graduate school; of its 116 students in 1970-71, 93 were at the graduate level. Technically a private *universidad libre* with its own degree-granting power, El Colegio began in 1938 not as a school but as a private-supported, public-assisted agency to help Spanish refugees from the Civil War in continuing their intellectual pursuits in Mexico. Today, the College receives the bulk of its funds from the Federal government (about two-thirds of its $1,250,000-plus annual budget) with assistance from the Banco de México, other public financial intermediaries, and foreign foundations.[7] For this reason the Colegio de México is more like a public than a private institution, and for the remainder of this book it will be treated as such.

Growth, Public and Private Universities

Total enrollments in Mexican universities and a breakdown of these enrollments by private and public sectors have been presented in Chapter Three. The figures given were for the year 1970-71 only, and it will be of interest to analyze the growth of the universities over several years.

The most complete data series available for higher education in the early 1960's is the ANUIES special series over the years 1959-1964 which was the presidential term of Adolfo López Mateos.[8] Although these data refer to the professional schools only (they do not include *prepas* or graduate schools), the data indicate substantial growth in university enrollments during the years considered (an average annual growth rate of 10.2 percent) and particularly strong growth in enrollments in the private universities.

In 1959 there were some 71,500 students in all of Mexico's professional schools, and only a little over ten percent of these students (some 7400) were in private universities. By 1964, however, the total number of students had risen to nearly 117,000, but now fifteen percent (17,400) of these students were entered in private schools. Whereas the growth in public university students over the five-year period was about 55 percent, or an average annual growth rate of 9.1 percent, in the private sector there were 137 percent more students in 1964 than in 1959, or an average annual growth rate of 18.8 percent. Thus the growth of the private professional schools more than doubled that of the public ones.

The relative concentration of educational infrastructure in Mexico City has been commented upon in Chapter Three. In the ANUIES data for 1959-1964, however, there appears a counter-tendency to this concentration, or perhaps merely a catching-up of the provinces with respect to higher education facilities. While inscriptions in universities in the Federal District increased at an average annual growth rate of 7.4 percent between 1959 and 1964, in the provinces they were up more than twice that, 15.8 percent yearly.

The figures of the above paragraph hide an important fact. While enrollments in public universities follow the trend above with respect to capitol and provincial growth, the private ones do not. Growth in private sector inscriptions between 1959 and 1964 was particularly pronounced in the capitol where enrollments increased from 4200 to nearly 11,000, or at an average rate of 20.8 percent per year.[9] Of course, the public institutions predominate numerically so that in total numbers the trends in the public sector prevail. Nevertheless, it is interesting to see that over this period the interests of the private sector have not matched public sector goals with regard to decentralization of university attendance in the capitol city.

Some further comments are in order about the 1959-1964 growth data. First, the ANUIES data from these years relate to professional school enrollments only and do not include graduate schools or, more importantly, *prepas*. More inclusive data are not available for these years as regards the other enrollment components of public and private universities. This is unfortunate because it has been previously noted from another source[10] that public *prepa* enrollment was increasing much faster than private enrollment between the years 1964 and 1970. Moreover, this aggregated data (from the Secretaría de Educación Pública) tends to contradict the 1959-1964 ANUIES data because it indicates that public and private professional schools were growing at about the same rate, with a slight edge for the *public* institutions.

A clue to this apparent contradiction can be found in the disaggregated ANUIES data from 1967-1971, the only five years for which complete university enrollment data are currently available. During these years total public university enrollment has increased more than private enrollment, the reverse of the earlier 1959-1964 trend, with public universities growing at a 12.8 percent average annual rate where the private institutions' enrollment increased at 11.5 percent. (See Table 4-1.) Apparently the burst of private enrollment that occurred between 1959 and 1964 has slowed down in recent years, so that later data would show faster growth of the public schools. With regard to professional schools only, data from 1967-1971 shows public enrollments growing faster than private ones (14.4 percent and 13.0 percent), again the reverse of the 1959-1964 trend.

As to the *prepas*, the aggregated Secretariat of Public Education data include, for example for 1970, some 6,600 public and 35,000 private *prepa* students that are outside of universities, i.e. in public or private preparatory schools that do not provide professional level training as well. Given these differences in quantities, it is not possible to infer university connected *prepa* trends from the aggregated data for the years 1964-1970. The only data avalable, then, concerning university *prepas* are those of ANUIES for the years 1967-1971, and these data indicate that public *prepa* enrollment in universities was growing considerably faster across these years than was private enrollment.[11]

For the years 1967-1971, enrollment figures and growth information are presented in Table 4-1. Total university enrollment has been growing at an average annual rate of about twelve-and-a-half percent. Graduate school enrollment has been advancing the fastest over the five years, and university professional schools have grown faster than the *prepas*. Overall enrollment increases in the States (at an average rate of 12.8 percent) have about kept pace with those in the Federal District (12.5 percent). The tendency has been for the public universities in the Federal District to grow faster than those in the States, and the opposite is true with regard to the private institutions. In this case, the private university sector has complied with government decentralization policies better than the public sector.

The Private Universities, Some Measures

Turning now to the private universities, from the total number (47)[12] of these institutions in the nation in 1970-71, Table 4-2 gives a picture of the twelve largest by student enrollment.

Of the remaining 35 private institutions not listed in Table 4-2, none had more than 1,000 students registered in 1970-71 and 28 of the 35 had fewer than five hundred students in total.[13] Most private schools are very small, indeed, and an important insight into private higher education appears: in 1970-71 there were only twelve private institutions in the Republic with over a thousand students, and the very largest of these (Autonomous University of Guadalajara) was dwarfed sixteen to one by the largest public university (UNAM).

The remaining universities were almost miniscule in comparison to the large public universities, particularly those of the Federal Dstrict.

Again, private universities demonstrate the same Mexico polarity that was seen with regard to universities in general, but to a slightly lesser degree. (See Table 3-4). Of the total of 47 private universities, 21 are in the Federal District. These 21 universities have a total enrollment of 25 thousand students, or about 49 percent of the total private enrollment of the country. (See Table 4-1.)

In Table 4-2, those universities checked, seven of twelve, are located in the capitol. Although the majority of important private universities are located in Mexico City, the largest of them are not in the capitol but in Guadalajara and Monterrey.

However, outside of Mexico City, Guadalajara, and Monterrey, few private students are to be found. In addition to the Autonomous University, Guadalajara contains a Jesuit-oriented institution of nearly 1,000 students, the Western Technological Institute of Higher Studies, and a smaller private higher normal school.

In Monterrey, besides the Monterrey Technological Institute, there are six other private universities, three of which are listed in Table 4-2. This leaves in the rest of the Republic only fourteen other private universities scattered about in various of the more important Mexican cities, as indicated in Table 4-3. Table 4-3 shows once more the tendency to centralization that is a part of Mexican society and is reflected in its educational infrastructure. Outside of the main cities of the Republic, fewer than 5,000 students attend private schools, or about eight percent of the private school total, and less than one percent of the total university enrollment across the country.

Quality Considerations

The private universities of Mexico enjoy far greater prestige than their number and sizes would indicate. In the "conventional wisdom" the private universities are believed to produce the "best" college graduates in the Republic. This applies particularly with regard to the larger of the private institutions, but the impression spreads to many of the smaller ones as well.

TABLE 4-1

PUBLIC AND PRIVATE UNIVERSITY ENROLLMENTS, 1966-67 TO 1970-71

	1966-67		1967-68		1968-69		1969-70		1970-71	
	Total	%	Total	%	Total	%	Total	%	Total	%
No. of universities										
public	67	63	73	65	72	63	76	64	78	62
private	38	37	39	35	42	37	42	36	47	38
Total	103	100	112	100	114	100	118	100	125	100
No. of students										
Prepas										
public	115,305	92	133,494	92	131,117	91	139,929	92	172,435	93
private	10,354	8	12,303	8	12,758	9	12,516	8	13,816	7
Total	125,659	100	145,797	100	143,875	100	152,445	100	186,251	100
Professional schools										
public	128,480	85	143,659	85	165,483	86	188,654	86	220,347	86
private	22,336	15	25,343	15	25,865	14	29,983	14	36,405	14
Total	150,816	100	169,002	100	191,348	100	218,637	100	256,752	100
Graduate schools										
public	2,566	89	3,257	85	4,342	87	4,960	86	5,631	87
private	332	11	556	15	670	13	793	14	830	13
Total	2,898	100	3,813	100	5,012	100	5,753	100	6,461	100

TABLE 4-1 (Continued)

PUBLIC AND PRIVATE UNIVERSITY ENROLLMENTS, 1966-67 TO 1970-71

	1966-67 Total	%	1967-68 Total	%	1968-69 Total	%	1969-70 Total	%	1970-71 Total	%
All levels										
public	246,351	88	280,410	88	300,942	88	333,543	89	398,413	89
private	33,022	12	38,202	12	39,293	12	43,292	11	51,051	11
Total	279,373	100	318,612	100	340,235	100	376,835	100	449,464	100
TOTAL ENROLLMENTS:										
Federal District										
public	133,419	87	148,002	87	165,542	88	178,827	89	219,851	90
private	19,439	13	22,362	13	22,787	12	22,558	11	24,864	10
Total	152,858	100	170,364	100	188,329	100	201,385	100	244,715	100
States										
public	112,932	89	132,408	89	135,347	89	154,716	88	178,562	87
private	13,583	11	15,840	11	16,559	11	20,734	12	26,187	13
Total	126,515	100	148,248	100	151,906	100	175,450	100	204,749	100

TABLE 4-1 (Continued)

PUBLIC AND PRIVATE UNIVERSITY ENROLLMENTS, 1966-67 TO 1970-71

AVERAGE ANNUAL GROWTH RATES, *1967-1971*

Total enrollment:	12.6%	*Prepas* only:	10.3%
public	12.6	public	10.6
private	11.5	private	7.5
Federal District:	12.5%	Professional schools only: 14.2%	
public	13.3	public	14.4
private	6.3	private	13.0
States:	12.8%	Graduate schools only: 22.1%	
public	10.5	public	21.7
private	17.8	private	25.7

Note: Figures in this Table differ slightly from those of Table 3-1 in that El Colegio de México is here considered a public university.

Source: Asociación Nacional de Universidades e Institutos de Enseñanza Superior, *La Enseñanza Superior en México*, 1967 through 1971 editions, *passim*.

TABLE 4-2

ENROLLMENTS, LARGEST PRIVATE MEXICAN UNIVERSITIES, 1970-71

		No. students, all levels*
1.	Autonomous University of Guadalajara	8,328
2.	Monterrey Technological Institute	6,599
†3.	Iberoamerican University	5,026
†4.	LaSalle University	4,301
†5.	University of the Valley of Mexico	3,587
†6.	Higher Institute for Commercial Studies	2,556
7.	Center for University Studies (Monterrey)	2,206
8.	University of Monterrey	1,725
†9.	School of Banking and Commerce	1,623
10.	Regiomontana University (Monterrey)	1,552
†11.	Technological University of Mexico	1,512
12.	Autonomous Technological Institute of Mexico	1,124

* *Prepas*, professional schools, graduate schools

† Located in Mexico City.

Source: ANUIES, *La Enseñanza Superior en México*, 1971, pp. 29ff.

TABLE 4-3

ENROLLMENTS, PRIVATE UNIVERSITIES IN SELECTED MEXICAN CITIES, 1970-71

City	No. private Universities		Total enrollment*
Ciudad Juárez, Chihuahua	2		859
León, Guanajuato	3		786
Mexicali, Baja California	1		671
Saltillo, Coahuila	2		662
Oaxaca, Oaxaca	1	(higher normal school)	643
Monclova, Coahuila	1		294
San Luis Potosí, S.L.P.	1		182
Uruapan, Michoacán	1	(higher normal school)	99
Puebla, Puebla	1	(higher normal school)	98
Piedras Negras, Coahuila	1		18
Totals	14		4312

* Prepas, professional schools, graduate schools

Source: ANUIES, La Enseñanza Superior en México, 1971, pp. 29ff.

The conventional wisdom was informally tested in this case by interviews with persons — professional educators, U.S. Embassy and Consular officials, and others — who could be considered to be well informed with respect to Mexican higher education. While results were not unanimous, it was clear that some of the larger private universities — Monterrey Technological Institute and the Iberoamerican University were named most frequently — were thought to be consistent producers of quality graduates. The UNAM was also named, and also less frequently the IPN. The general view with regard to the latter two, in keeping with the conclusion of Charles N. Myers,[14] was that in the mass of students that attend these institutions, they produce both very good and very poor graduates and all manner of gradations between these two extremes. Mentioned most frequently as a limiting factor in the provision of quality education in the state and federal universities were the frequent political unheavals that occur in the public institutions. These political disturbances take a particular form in Mexico, and more will be said about them in Chapter Five.

More than one interviewee mentioned, too, the fact that considerable human resources are available to the large federal universities in the capitol as opposed to the state universities in the provinces. Given the fact that most of the best qualified Mexicans in all fields are working in Mexico City, there is a large pool of part-time and full-time talent available to these institutions. This is not so, however, in the provinces, as was intimated by the discussions in this and the previous chapter of the capitol-provincial dichotomy. Nor do financial resources in the provinces match those in Mexico City. For example, Table 4-4 presents the per-student total governmental expenditures by region of the public institutions who are members of ANUIES, and are the largest and best established universities in the nation. The universities of the capitol receive subsidies considerably higher than those of most state institutions. The set of universities next closest are those of the northwest and north. In the south central, southeast and central areas, appropriations are very low, indeed, less than one-fourth the average of those of the capitol.

A measure of the quality preference for universities, at least in business fields, was attempted as part of other research carried out by the author.[15] A questionnaire was mailed to a number of businessmen in Guadalajara who had been identified, on the basis of a previous questionnaire, to be highly-paid holders of important positions in their firms. These businessmen were asked, among other things, to rank public and private institutions as to the quality of their students and the degree to which they would be willing to pay more to hire a new candidate for employment who had graduated from any particular institution, public or private.

The respondees were asked to rank a mixed group of ten public and private universities known to enjoy the highest prestige in Mexico.[16] Of these ten universities Monterrey Technological Institute received the most "votes" with respect to the quality of its student output, followed by the Iberoamerican University and by UNAM.

TABLE 4-4

ALL GOVERNMENT EXPENDITURES PER STUDENT
IN PUBLIC UNIVERSITIES* BY REGION 1970-71

Region	Universities	Expenditures per student ($U.S.)
Federal District	UNAM, IPN, El Colegio de México	$427
Northwest	Autonomous Universities of Baja California, Chihuahua, Sinaloa, Technological Institute of Sonora, University of Sonora	244
North	Autonomous Universities of Nuevo León, Tamaulipas, University of Coahuila	239
South	Institute of Science and Arts of Chiapas, "Benito Juárez" University of Oaxaca, Autonomous "Juárez" University of Tabasco, University of Veracruz	193
West	Universities of Colima, Guanajuato, Guadalajara, Michoacán, Nayarit	138
South Central	Autonomous Universities of Guerrero, Hidalgo, State of México, State of Morelos, Puebla	125
Southeast	University of the Southeast in Campeche, University of Yucatán	102
Central	Science and Technology Institute of Aguascalientes, "Juárez" University of Durango, Autonomous Universities of Querétaro, San Luis Potosí, Zacatecas	94

* Includes student enrollment at all levels. Member universities of ANUIES only.

Source: ANUIES, La Enseñanza Superior en México, 1971, pp. 29ff., 283.

The Autonomous University of Guadalajara and the National Polytechnic ranked next. Most of the respondees also indicated they would pay higher starting salaries to graduates of these same universities.[17]

With regard to this continued emphasis on the Monterrey Technological Institute, it is interesting to note that in Richard King's work on the provincial universities of Mexico, Monterrey Technological was the only private university in King's sample of nine of the "largest and best established of the provincial universities."[18] Yet in a large majority of the quality measures presented by King, the Institute ranked at or near the top, namely in publishing and graduate study by professors, library services and facilities, programs for upgrading of faculty, and others. In light of this information, it is not surprising that businessmen would prefer to hire graduates from this university, and that public opinion would put Monterrey Technological at the head of the list of quality universities.

In sum, it appears that the Mexican private universities enjoy a position of importance in Mexican higher education in terms of the quality of that system. The rest of this chapter will attempt to present some understanding of the preeminence that the private institutions and their graduates enjoy.

The King Report

First of all, in his path-breaking book on Mexican higher education in the provinces, Richard King tries to identify some of the variables that impinge on quality in the provincial universites. King's study is not a comparative one as between public and private Universities since all but one of King's sample institutions are public.[19]

King, as an educator, deals with educational kinds of variables such as curriculum flexibility, professorial training, recruiting, and promotion of teaching personnel, library holdings and services, research in progress, and others. A further discussion of more economic variables will follow in the next section.

With regard to curriculum, King finds that among the provincial universities, curricula tend to be rigid, ". . . with few options and few possibilities for transfer of credit from one faculty or one program to another."[20] Students enter specialization in the very first semester of their careers. The careers themselves tend to be fairly fixed as to courses leading to the degree, and only rarely may a student take a course in another career. Likewise, an interchange of professors between different schools of the university does not ordinarily take place. Thus the schools tend to be isolated from each other. Students take the courses prescribed by their school, and they are taught only by instructors of the profession to which they aspire. Only infrequently are they exposed to interdisciplinary training. The concept of a liberal arts curriculum for all students is a U.S. invention which did not take hold in Mexico.

It deserves mention here apart from the King Report, that three of the top private universities — Monterrey Technological Institute, the Iberoamerican University, and the Autonomous University of Guadalajara — have initiated "departmentalization" programs wherein basic courses are offered across fields. Thus duplication of these courses in different schools is avoided (leading to cost savings) and, in particular, students receive courses from professors especially trained in the subject matter.[21] It is also to be noted that the use of *"años comunes"* or "common years" where all students receive the same basic courses, is growing in Mexico. This is an innovation akin to departmentalization with some of the same advantages. In 1970-71 some 10,500 students were enrolled in *años comunes* in various fields, notably business and engineering. Most of these students (54 percent) were in Mexico City at the National Polytechnic.

Further, King points out, changes in curricula and programs of study that do occur tend to be ". . . administrative changes that do not substantially alter the nature of the studies themselves."[22] New careers may be added, or new courses, but seldom is new methodology introduced or is the content of a career changed to reflect new, practical, or research findings. In short, curriculum planning, such as it is, tends to be tradition-bound among the universities, with regard to program content as well as cross-training across careers. "In most cases," King points out, "changes in programs of study are simply the addition or rearrangement of courses without an attempt to reorient the student's approach to learning."[23]

Concerning the training, recruiting, and promotion of university professors, King finds that most instructors are relatively young: half of the respondees to his questionnaires were about thirty years old. Thus one can expect that the level of training of these teachers would be limited, and King's data bear this out: no more than eleven percent of his 327 sample teachers had master's degrees, and only five percent had doctorates. Nearly forty percent, however, had undertaken some post-graduate study.

The youth of faculty members is characteristic all over Mexico, among private as well as public institutions. Faculty training is a problem wihch extends beyond Mexico to Central America[24] and farther south. Universities in Latin America have difficulty in recruiting mature and highly-trained professionals because of low salary limits and fairly uniform pay scales regardless of age, experience, and training. For the same reason, there is little incentive for the professor to continue his training even though he may be highly motivated to teach. As King points out:

> . . . it must be noted that incentives for graduate study, including the promise of professional advancement upon receipt of the master's or doctor's degree, do not exist for either full-time or part-time professors.[25]

More will be said about economic incentives in the next section of this chapter, but it should be noted here that of all the measures presented by King which show differences between the public provincial universities and the lone private institution, Monterrey Technological Institute, it is in faculty training that the Institute stands out most; whereas the next highest university had eleven percent of its faculty possessing master's degrees, the Institute had 41 percent holding the degree. With regard to doctorates, the Institute again led the way with nineteen percent of its professors possessing the degree. Evidently, there is a substantial difference in Monterrey Technological's ability to attract and keep more highly trained instructional personnel. At least part of this difference will be examined more closely in a moment with respect to the University of Nuevo León, one of the Institute's principal competitors.

Libraries are another important aspect of university education and another source of difficulty for the public universities in King's sample. Although all but one of King's public institutions had a central library, it appears that small libraries in universities' individual schools are more important than the central libraries. Holdings are very limited in these small facilities. The median number of volumes was 1300, and ninety percent of the schools held fewer than 5000 books. Only two of the public universities, King reports, indicate systematic use of services such as information about new books, reserve shelving, circulation privileges for students, and acquisition of new books on professors' recommendations.

Finally, with respect to research emphasis at the provincial universities, apparently there have been some efforts to enlarge the institutions' participation in research projects, particularly within university-sponsored research institutes. However, it is not clear that this research then becomes a part of the teaching program, and independent research projects carried out by individual faculty members are low in number. In the concluding chapter of King's book[26] appears the flat statement that "very little research" is done in the provincial universities. Some few deans (eleven of 66) did report positive incentives of various sorts for research productivity, academic promotion and reduced teaching loads being the most important.[27] But according to the responses of the great majority of deans, incentives for faculty to engage in research were nil. This result is not surprising given the low number of doctorates among the university faculties and the lack of effective promotion possibilities for whatever reason.[28]

In sum, the provincial universities appear to have what one might identify as "growing pains." One would expect that in a developing country like Mexico, educational infrastructure would still be in process of development. What King's analysis does is to identify some of the problem areas in Mexican higher education and indicate that the institutions which enjoy higher prestige probably fare better on one or more of King's measures. Certainly Monterrey Technological Institute does.

Some Economic Considerations

Turning now to some economic measures, some further light may be shed on the quality question as between public and private uni-

TABLE 4-5

EXPENDITURES OF REPORTING PRIVATE UNIVERSITIES 1970-71

Region		Name	Total student body, all levels incl. secondary	Expenditures ($U.S.)		
				Total $000	Per student	Aver. for Region
Northwest	1.	Centro de Enseñanza Técnica y Superior; Mexicali, B. C.	671	$481.8	718	532
	2.	Universidad Autónoma de Ciudad Juárez, Cd. Juárez, Chih.	457	53.4	117	
	3.	Escuela Superior de Agricultura, "Hnos. Escobar," Cd. Juárez, Chih.	402	179.2	446	
	4.	Universidad Militarizada de México; Hermosillo, Son.	287	251.4	876	
North	5.	Escuela de Ingeniería Mecánica y Eléctrica; Monclova, Coah.	294	64.5	219	470
	6.	Instituto de Estudios Profesionales de Saltillo; Saltillo, Coah.	534	35.5	66	
	7.	Facultades Universitarias de Saltillo; Saltillo, Coah.	128	32.0	250	
	8.	Instituto Tecnológico y de Estudios Superiores de Monterrey; Monterrey, Nuevo León	9,626	6,371.7	662	
	9.	Universidad Regiomontana; Monterrey, N.L.	1,552	234.3	151	
	10.	Instituto Superior de Cultura y Arte de Monterrey; Monterrey, N.L.	30	18.5	617	
	11.	Universidad de Monterrey; Monterrey, N.L.	1,725	771.2	447	
	12.	Colegio Labastida; Monterrey, N.L.	60	14.7*	245	
	13.	Centro de Estudios Universitarios; Monterrey, N.L.	3,004	420.5*	140	

TABLE 4-5 (Continued)
EXPENDITURES OF REPORTING PRIVATE UNIVERSITIES 1970-71

Region	Name	Total student body, all levels incl. secondary	Expenditures ($U.S.)		
			Total $000	Per student	Aver. for Region
Center	14. Instituto Tecnológico y de Estudios Superiores Potosino, San Luis Potosí, S.L.P.	231	37.2	161	161
West	15. Escuela Profesional de Comercio y Administración; León, Gto.	468	56.4	120	
	16. Instituto América, León, Gto.	978	26.2	27	
	17. Universidad Autónoma de Guadalajara; Guadalajara, Jal.	9,011	5935.5	659	
	18. Escuela Normal Superior Nueva Galicia; Guadalajara, Jal.	295	60.0	203	566
	19. Instituto Tecnológico y de Estudios Superiores del Occidente, Guadalajara, Jal.	1,023	591.6	578	
Center South	20. Escuela Normal Superior Benavente; Puebla, Pue.	98	18.5	189	189
Southeast	NONE				
	NONE				
Federal District	21. Universidad Femenina de México	599	†	†	
	22. Universidad Iberoamericana	5,026	3257.7	648	
	23. Universidad Tecnológica de México	1,512	138.1	91	
	24. Escuela de Contabilidad y Administración de la Cd. de México	473	66.5	141	

TABLE 4-5 (Continued)

EXPENDITURES OF REPORTING PRIVATE UNIVERSITIES 1970-71

Region		Name	Total student body, all levels incl. secondary	Expenditures ($U.S.)		
				Total $000	Per student	Aver. for Region
Federal District (cont.)	25.	Instituto Panamericano de Humanidades	122	59.8	490	$318
	26.	Instituto Superior de Estudios Comerciales	2,714	574.7	212	
	27.	Escuela Normal Superior "FEP"	667	30.8	46	
	28.	Instituto de Cultura	106	21.2*	200	
	29.	Colegio Español de México	874	3.2	4	
	30.	Escuela Libre de Derecho	427	33.8	79	
	31.	Escuela de Ingeniería Municipal	245	41.8	171	
	32.	Instituto de Ciencias Sociales, Económicas y Administrativas	629	86.1	137	
	33.	Instituto Tecnológico Autónomo de México	1,124	888.6	791	
	34.	Escuela Libre de Homeopatía de México	238	18.9*	79	
	35.	Universidad del Valle de México	3,587	†	†	

TOTAL STUDENTS   49,217

TOTAL EXPENDITURES $21,495,300

NATIONAL AVERAGE EXPENDITURES PER STUDENT, PRIVATE UNIVERSITIES $437

* Incomes only reported.   † Confidential data, included in totals

Source: ANUIES, *La Enseñanza Superior en México, 1971, passim.*

versities. A major indicator would certainly be per-student expenditures. If more resources are allocated to one or the other of the kinds of institutions, a higher quality output may be expected to result.

Income-expenditure levels at 35 of the 47 private institutions can be examined using a combination of ANUIES and original data gathered at the universities. Among these 35 are ten of the twelve largest private universities,[29] and all of the private universities which enjoy high prestige in Mexico. The average per-student expenditures among these universities in the 1970-71 school year was $437. The range of expenditures among the universities can be seen in Table 4-5.

It is not a surprising result that the institutions mentioned earlier in quality context spend more than the average amount. Monterrey Technological Institute (No. 8 in the table), for example, spent $662 per student in 1970-71, the Autonomous University of Guadalajara (No. 17) $659, and the Iberoamerican University (No. 22) $648. Two smaller institutions, the Center for Technical and Higher Learning in Mexicali (No. 1) and the Autonomous Technological Institute of Mexico (No. 33), spent larger amounts than either of the foregoing universities.

Only eight of the 35 private universities spent more than $500 per student in 1970-71; two of these were in the Federal District, four in the north and northwest, and two in the west. Almost half of the reporting institutions were in the Federal District, as might be expected. As an aside, a surprising fact shown in Table 4-5 is the character of per-student expenditures in capitol and in province. The private sector tendency seems to be the reverse of that of the public sector; per-student expenditures by private universities in the provinces are considerably more than those of the capitol. In the fifteen reporting universities of the provinces, average per-student expenditures were about $507 whereas in the thirteen reporting universities in Mexico City they were only about $318. Even if the two top spending provincial universities are removed from these totals (ITESM and UAG) one still finds that average per-student expenditure in the States are nearly as high as those in the capitol — $261 as opposed to $285. Again it is seen that private sector policy has not matched that of

TABLE 4-6

EXPENDITURES OF REPORTING PUBLIC UNIVERSITIES 1970-71

Region		Name	Total student body, all levels incl. secondary	Expenditures ($U.S.)		
				Total $000	Per student	Aver. for Region
Northwest	1.	Universidad Autónoma de Baja California	4,383	1622.5	370	
	2.	Universidad Autónoma de Chihuahua	6,132	1359.0	222	
	3.	Instituto Tecnológico Regional de Cd. Juárez	1,032	636.2*	616	
	4.	Escuela Normal Superior "Prof. José E. Medrano"	20	3.1*	155	333
	5.	Universidad Autónoma de Sinaloa	5,407	2063.7	382	
	6.	Universidad de Sonora	6,513	2334.2	358	
	7.	Instituto Tecnológico de Sonora	1,233	224.5	182	
North	8.	Universidad de Coahuila	9,646	2203.2	228	
	9.	Instituto Tecnológico Regional de Coahuila	1,312	485.6	370	
	10.	Instituto Tecnológico Regional de la Laguna	1,327	115.2*	87	
	11.	Universidad Autónoma de Nuevo León	22,728	5890.3	259	245
	12.	Escuela Normal Superior del Estado de Nuevo León	1,834	264.3	144	
	13.	Universidad Autónoma de Tamaulipas	4,820	1554.8	323	
	14.	Instituto Tecnológico Regional de Cd. Madero	2,166	125.8*	58	
	15.	Instituto Tecnológico Regional de Nuevo Laredo	338	184.4	546	
Center	16.	Instituto Autónomo de Ciencias y Tecnología, Aguascalientes	1,350	295.3	219	
	17.	Instituto Tecnológico Regional de Aguascalientes	865	295.3	341	
	18.	Universidad "Juárez" del Estado de Durango	2,938	483.3	165	

TABLE 4-6 (Continued)

EXPENDITURES OF REPORTING PUBLIC UNIVERSITIES 1970-71

Region		Name	Total student body, all levels incl. secondary	Expenditures ($U.S.)		
				Total $000	Per student	Aver. for Region
Center (cont.)	19.	Instituto Tecnológico Regional de Durango	1,266	116.5	92	
	20.	Universidad Autónoma de Querétaro	2,563	318.5	124	
	21.	Instituto Tecnológico Regional de Querétaro	986	32.2	33	148
	22.	Universidad Autónoma de San Luis Potosí	8,779	966.3	110	
	23.	Universidad Autónoma de Zacatecas	2,671	663.4*	248	
West	24.	Universidad de Colima	1,374	198.4	144	
	25.	Universidad de Guanajuato	6,218	1838.6	296	
	26.	Instituto Tecnológico Regional de Celaya	1,044	463.0	443	
	27.	Escuela Normal Superior del Estado de Guanajuato	176	22.5*	128	166
	28.	Universidad de Guadalajara	35,178	5279.9	150	
	29.	Universidad Michoacana de San Nicolás de Hidalgo	10,469	1382.6	132	
	30.	Universidad de Nayarit	2,922	254.6	87	
	31.	Escuela Normal Superior del Estado de Nayarit	65	78.0	1200	
Center South	32.	Universidad Autónoma de Guerrero	3,413	718.0	210	
	33.	Universidad Autónoma de Hidalgo	2,591	278.6	108	195
	34.	Universidad Autónoma del Edo. de México	6,299	1900.0*	302	
	35.	Escuela Normal Superior del Edo. de México	378	82.8	219	

TABLE 4-6 (Continued)

EXPENDITURES OF REPORTING PUBLIC UNIVERSITIES 1970-71

Region	Name	Total student body, all levels incl. secondary	Expenditures ($U.S.)		
			Total $000	Per student	Aver. for Region
	36. Escuela Nacional de Agricultura, Chapingo	1,527	1056.7*	692	
	37. Universidad Autónoma del Edo. de Morelos	4,609	522.9	113	
	38. Universidad Autónoma de Puebla	13,064	1853.9	142	
	39. Instituto de Estudios Superiores del Edo. de Tlaxcala	1,526	85.9	56	
South	40. Instituto de Ciencias y Artes de Chiapas	2,942	325.1	110	
	41. Escuela de Derecho San Cristobal Las Casas, Chiapas	279	16.6	59	
	42. Universidad "Benito Juárez" de Oaxaca	3,304	454.4	138	
	43. Universidad Autónoma "Juárez" de Tabasco	3,281	482.2	147	
	44. Colegio Superior de Agricultura Tropical de Tabasco	9	181.9	20211†	215
	45. Instituto Tecnológico Regional de Orizaba	1,525	28.6	19	
	46. Universidad Veracruzana	10,662	2826.3	265	
Southeast	47. Escuela Naval Militar	460	535.9	1165	
	48. Universidad del Sudeste, Campeche	859	232.6	271	
	49. Universidad de Yucatán	3,844	533.8	139	163
Federal District	50. UNAM	138,389	63434.8	458	
	51. IPN	83,474	36384.1	436	
	52. Escuela Nacional de Antropología e Historia	339	4739.5	13980	

TABLE 4-6 (Continued)

EXPENDITURES OF REPORTING PUBLIC UNIVERSITIES 1970-71

Region	Name	Total student body, all levels incl. secondary	Expenditures ($U.S.)		Aver. for Region
			Total $000	Per student	
	53. Centro de Investigaciones y de Estudios Avanzados del IPN	118	2021.2	17129‡	
	54. El Colegio de México**	116	1366.8	11783	
	55. Escuela Nacional de Biblioteconomía y Archivonomía	214	78.5	367	
	56. Escuela Normal Superior	1,729	467.2	270	487
	57. Escuela Normal de Especialización	249	6.0	24	
	58. Escuela Médico Militar	278	128.1*	461	
	59. Escuela Militar de Ingenieros	41	176.4*	4302	
	60. Escuela Superior de Guerra	103	321.9*	3125	
	61. Escuela de Salud Pública	152	531.3	3495	

TOTAL STUDENTS 433,619
TOTAL EXPENDITURES ($U.S.) $153,527,600
NATIONAL AVERAGE EXPENDITURES PER STUDENT, PUBLIC UNIVERSITIES $354

* incomes only reported
† new in 1969
‡ services IPN
** nominally private

Source: ANUIES, *La Enseñanza Superior en México, 1971, passim.*

the public sector; in this case, the private trend has been toward decentralization of educational infrastructure expenditures.

With regard to regional distribution, the last column of Table 4-5 shows the average per student expenditure of the universities by their respective regions (ANUIES classification). Average expenditures are highest in the north, northwest, and west, and lower in other areas, including the Federal District.

Turning now to the public sector, Table 4-6 lists the sixty-one public universities that reported their expenditures to ANUIES in 1970-71.[30]

The outstanding datum which draws attention in this table is overall per-student expenditures. The nationwide average for the public universities in 1970-71 was $354 per student, or nineteen percent less than was spent per pupil in the private institutions. It appears that relatively more resources per student are available for private than for public higher education.

In Table 4-6, it may also be noted that of the twelve universities which spent $500 or more per student, six are in the capital, not counting the UNAM itself which is very close to $500. Distribution of per-student expenditures between capitol and province is what would be expected from the earlier discussion, and the opposite of the private case above. Average per-student expenditures among universities of the capitol was $487, more than 2.3 times that of the province, which was $210 per student.

A regional analysis of per-student expenditures also gives results similar to those of Table 4-4. Outside the Federal District, expenditures are highest in the Northwest and North ($333 and $245) and lowest in West, Southeast, and Central parts of the nation ($166, $163, and $148). This pattern is similar to that of the private universities in Table 4-5, with the exception of the Federal District, as already noted, and in the West, where there are important private universities, principally in Guadalajara.

The fact that private universities spend more per student than public ones will be familiar to those who are acquainted with the expenditure picture of United States institutions. For 1970, data from the *Statistical Abstract of the United States, 1971,* puts per student annual expenditures for public universities at $2558 and for private universities at $4043, a 37 percent difference. The results of a recent Carnegie Commission study also stress this fact, e.g., instructional costs were higher in private than in public universities over the entire period from 1930-1967.[31]

Apart from quality considerations, why else might expeditures be higher in private schools? For the United States, explanations have been offered on a variety of grounds.[32]

1. Private institutions have higher costs for some purposes than do public ones, for example, recruitment of students, which public institutions generally have not been obliged to do.
2. Private institutions feel compelled to make increasing amounts of student aid available to compensate for high and rising tuitions.
3. At many private schools there is a larger percentage of graduate students in the student body mix, thus raising per-student costs.
4. Because of generally smaller size of private universities (private institutions average one-third the size of public ones in the U.S.) there may be increased costs due to diseconomies of scale.

In Mexico, some or all of the above considerations might be important in determining the higher per-student costs among the private universities, and it will be important to review them before making further comments about the meaning of the higher costs.

First, it must be mentioned here that student recruitment is a yet unpracticed art among public or private universities in Mexico. Very little has been done to make prospective students aware of enrollment benefits or programs available (recall traditional emphasis of careers), no mail campaigns are conducted, and university personnel hired to visit high schools (or *secundarias,* in this case) is unheard of. Apparently the boom of university attendance in the last decade has not forced the institutions to adopt offensive methods for attracting students. However, it is true that most private universities publish some brochures and information materials, which the public universities less commonly do. These brochures, even at the largest private universities, would not approach the complexity of the material available to students at most U.S. universities. But nevertheless some material exists, hence costs might be thought to be somewhat higher at the private institutions for this reason.

Again, touching point two above, it might appear that, given the nominal tuition rates at the public universities, tuitions already constitute a one-way grant from government to students, so further student aid would not be as necessary or as important as among the private institutions.[33] Thus private institutions might be the ones who are forced to bear higher scholarship costs.

Analyzing the available comparative data, the first two hypotheses regarding higher costs might appear to be borne out. For example, in the ANUIES university expenditure data for 1970-71, there is an expenditure line[34] called "Difusión Cultural," which is described as "expenditures for . . . scholarships, conferences, theater, expositions, etc." If this item is used as a proxy and the aggregate per-student amounts spent by public and private institutions are calculated, it turns out that private schools spend twice as much per student as public ones do.[35] The amounts are fairly low in any case, $11 per student among the public universities and $22 among the private ones, so at the outside the difference, $11, would only be a fraction of the total difference of per-student costs (some 13 percent).

But if the Monterrey Technological Institute, far and away the biggest spender is excluded (the Technological spent some $68 per student in 1970-71 in this area), one finds that the public universities actually spend *more* than do the private ones on "Difusión Cultural." The dollar amounts are low in both sectors, $11 per student, in the public universities and about $7.50 in the private ones, so that comparisons become difficult. But the net result is that, except for Monterrey Technological, per student costs do not seem to be higher among the private universities due to recruitment and scholarship expenditures. If anything, the reverse tends to be true, although these costs are not very high at any university, public or private, for reasons discussed above. At the Monterrey Technological Institute the majority of these extra costs appear to be for scholarships, which have averaged $40 per student over the years 1969-1972 and in 1970-71 were as high as $47.[36]

Relating to the first hypothesis above, another fact appears in the ANUIES data, one which implies higher per student costs among the *public* universities, particularly among the larger public institutions, These universities have state and regional responsibilities for providing cultural and informational services which entail considerable expense, responsibilities which the private universities do not have. These expenditures run the gamut from, for example, the university theater and music groups at the Autonomous University of Sinaloa and the University of Veracruz to the museum and radio-TV department of the University of Sonora.

At these institutions this kind of expense may add up to $6 to $7 per student, which is as much as some private universities spend on "Difusión Cultural" in its entirety.

In any case, it does not appear that the private universities end up spending more on "Difusión Cultural," broadly stated. If anything, the costs for most private universities for recruiting and student aid would tend to be compensated by the social service costs implicit in the operation of the public university. Thus it is probably not true that higher expenditures exist for most Mexican private universities on a broad interpretation of the first two explanations given earlier.

As regards the third possible explanation for higher private university costs, more graduate students at the private institutions, this is definitely not true, as seen in Chapter Three. Graduate enrollment between public and private schools closely follows the pattern of total enrollment, public institutions claiming some 86 percent of the country's graduate students in 1970-71. Thus it might be said that costs cannot be higher among the private institutions due to graduate student load since the great majority of graduate students are in the public universities. This response, however, would gloss over some important facts among both the private and the public institutions.

The first is that all the graduate students enrolled in the private universities in 1970-71 attended no more than two of the universities, Monterrey Technological and Iberoamerican, which contained 635 and 195 students each, respectively, accounting for ten percent and four percent of each student body.[37] Likewise in the public sector, two universities, UNAM and the University of Nuevo León, account for some 80 percent of all 5,500-plus public graduate students (enrollments here were three percent and 2.5 percent of each student body.)

Referring now to Table 4-5, per-student costs are higher at Iberoamerican and at Monterrey Technological. Unfortunately it is not possible to associate these higher costs with either of the particular programs, given either the ANUIES data or the data available at the two institutions. Cost-accounting procedures simply do not offer any convenient way of breaking down resources assigned to graduate as opposed to undergraduate programs.[38] However, it is reasonable to assume that a part of these higher costs are due to the fledgling graduate programs at these institutions. At the public universities, the picture is not so clear. At UNAM, referring to Table 4-6, per-student costs are higher than the national average; however, at the University of Nuevo León, costs are lower than average even though there are some graduate students. At three institutions which have a large proportion of graduate students, Escuela Nacional de Agricultura (Chapingo), El Colegio de México, and IPN's Centro de Investigaciones y de Estudios Avanzados, costs are higher than average, considerably so in the latter two cases.

In sum, it may be said that, although it is most probable that graduate students and the ancillary programs which accompany their presence raise per student costs, private schools do not seem to incur these costs more than public ones. Moreover, if all the institutions containing graduate students are removed from the calculus, it is still true that private universities spend more per student than public ones, about ten percent more, and the necessity for accounting for these increased expenditures remains.

Finally, commenting upon the question of scale economies, a

glance at Tables 4-5 and 4-6 will convince the reader, if he has not already been amply persuaded earlier in the chapter, of the consequential size differences between public and private universities. The public universities in the tables average four times as large as the private ones. Moreover, there seems to be no consistent relationship between the size of the institution and per-student costs.[39] Of course, it would be a mistake to place heavy emphasis on comparisons of per-student costs as between universities on any particular variable like size. As the California and Western Conference has warned, crude comparisons of total costs or costs per student are useless without accompanying data on the difference in the factors affecting expenditures.[40]

Nevertheless, with this caution in mind, one may presume that the size of enrollment affects the cost structure of the institution,[41] and suppose that at least some of the difference in per-student costs between public and private universities is due to diseconomies of scale among the smaller private institutions. Unfortunately, no clear answer can be given here. However, of ten private universities interviewed by the author, all but two believed that they were in the downslope of their average cost curve, or that more students would bring increased efficiency of their other inputs. These universities interviewed all contained upwards of 750 students. The universities which believed their efficiency limits were being reached contained as many as 5,000 to 10,000 students and were beginning to limit their enrollment. This datum would indicate there are economies of scale over broad ranges of enrollment, depending on other factors such as plant size, numbers of courses (careers) offered, number of student shifts possible, and other variables. It is probable that the smaller private universities are operating suboptimally and that increased enrollment would lower per-student costs.

However, attention in Mexico today, particularly in the public sector, is being focused on the other side of the problem, namely diseconomies due to overcrowding. Given the rapid increases in university enrollment in the past decade, public universities are feeling the squeeze of students, and it is likely that many of them are operating at increased costs due to this overcrowding. This situation is particularly acute at the UNAM, which was originally designed for a maximum of some 50,000 students in some distant future and which in 1970-71 contained nearly triple that enrollment.

The overcrowding with respect to UNAM has some interesting implications with regard to planning. For a long period of time it was Mexico's dream to have an impressive national university campus to contain its growing number of students and also to take advantage of internal economies. Finally in the early 1950's the monumental *Ciudad Universitaria* was built, in the south of Mexico City, a tremendous effort which resulted in the striking campus that was Mexico's pride at the time. Unfortunately, subsequent overcrowding has changed the huge campus into a nightmare of cramped facilities, parking difficulties, and in addition such an agglomeration of students that a small spark can set off political demonstrations with national implications. IPN's Polytecnic City, somewhat smaller than University City, also has many more students than planned for, and the situation is the same in the larger provincial universities as well. The University of Guadalajara, for example, must turn away large numbers of its new applicants for admission every year for lack of space.

Thus, if some of the private universities face higher costs due to small size or diseconomies of scale, it is equally likely that many public universities face similar diseconomies because of an excess of students. Moreover, as population increases and greater demand for university education puts further pressure on existing university facilities, one may expect these diseconomies to tend to disappear for the growing private universities and to become more significant for the overburdened public institutions.

Much more research is needed here to determine the shape of the Mexican universities' cost function and the importance of the variables determining that function. But, in summary, it is not clearly demonstrable that private university costs are significantly higher for technical reasons or for reasons special to the universities' existence as private institutions. One is left trying to explain these higher costs on other grounds that concern the universities' provision of education services, i.e., quality considerations. An effort to deal with this question in economic terms is the subject of the next section.

Faculty Salaries

The most important item in the budgets of nearly all the ANUIES-reporting universities, is, as would be expected from the United States' experience, faculty salaries. Overall, this expenditure accounts for about forty percent of the reported outlays of the universities and represents the largest expenditure item in the ANUIES series.[42] In an analysis of faculty salaries, then, some differences may be encountered that will be enlightening as regards the allocation of human resources between public and private institutions and help to explain the higher levels of costs at the private universities.

A breakout of faculty salaries brings one face to face with a situation that is greatly different from the United States' with regard to university hiring practices. Most Mexican and other Latin American professors work on a part-time basis as an adjunct to their professional careers. Their university positions are held for prestige, or for contacts, and less frequently for reasons of income dependence. Sometimes the professor's teaching time is simply donated to the university. This characteristic of the so-called "taxi professor," is prevalent throughout Latin America and has been widely commented upon.[43] But for present purposes professors' salaries will be compared as between public and private universities, and thus not only must full-time salaries be analyzed, but also those of part-time professors with varying loads. For reasons of employment motive mentioned above, there is likely to be discontinuity between the different wage scales.

Table 4-7 attempts to present typical minimum monthly salaries paid to professors at the larger public and private universities in the three most important Mexican cities. The three most usual kinds of contracts are for full-time, roughly the equivalent of the professional arrangement in the U.S., half-time, a less common contract, and hourly, which is, as mentioned, the most common form of contract.

TABLE 4-7

FACULTY SALARIES, SELECTED MEXICAN CITIES, 1970-71

(All figures in Mexican Pesos — $1 peso = $0.8 dollar)

	Minimum average monthly salaries Full-time	Half-time	Average hourly rates for part-time professors
GUADALAJARA			
Public			
Universidad de Guadalajara	3425	--------	26
Private			
Universidad Autónoma de Guadalajara*	4000	--------	94
ITESO (Western Technological Institute)	7200	3000	30
MONTERREY			
Public			
Universidad de Nuevo León	4100	2600	49
Private			
ITESM (Monterrey Technological)	7450	2900	64
Universidad Regiomontana	4500	2500	51
Centro de Estudios Universitarios de Monterrey	--------	--------	49
Universidad de Monterrey	6000	3000	30
FEDERAL DISTRICT			
Public			
UNAM*	5600	3000	40
IPN*	6000	3000	35
Colegio de México	6000	4000	156
Private			
Universidad Iberoamericana	7160	3600	44
ITAM (Technological Institute of Mexico)	9000	5000	56
Escuela Bancaria y Comercial (School of Banking and Commerce)	--------	--------	43
Universidad Anáhuac	8000	4000	50

* Not reported to ANUIES

Source: ANUIES, *La Enseñanza Superior en México, 1971*, pp. 260ff.

The job descriptions of the hourly professors and the number of hours taught vary widely, so a class-hour wage rate is presented in the table.

Inter-city comparisons are eschewed so as to avoid cost-of-living differences, but within cities the private universities tend to pay more to their professors. With few exceptions the private universities in all three cities were paying higher salaries than their competing state university, at all contractual levels and particularly for full-time professors.

If this is so, then one would expect there to be more professors available to the students of private universities and particularly more full-time professors. The data bear out this supposition. In 1970-71 there were a total of about 39,300 university teachers in Mexico, and they were distributed between public and private universities as per Table 4-8.

If the percentages of Table 4-8 are compared with those of Table 3-1 of the last chapter, it is seen that the private universities had percentage-wise fewer students (11.4 percent) than teachers (13.8 percent), which means lower student/teacher ratios. Using the data from these two tables, average ratios for the two kinds of institutions can be calculated. In the public universities the figure is 11.7 to 1 and in the private universities 9.4 to 1.

TABLE 4-8
TOTAL PROFESSORS PUBLIC AND PRIVATE UNIVERSITIES,* 1970-71

	No. of professors	%
Public universities	33,927	86.2
Private universities	5,409	13.8
	39,336	100.0

*Prepas and above.

Source: ANUIES, La Enseñanza Superior en México, 1971, pp. 260ff.

In absolute values, of course, these figures are misleading since they include so many part-time professors. Of the time-classifiable (about 30,700) professors of Table 4-8, more than 26,000, or over 85 percent were teaching on an hourly basis. Another 1,600 (five percent) were half time, leaving about 2,750, or nine percent teaching full time. Thus the ratio of students to full-time-equivalent professors for Mexico will be much higher than the figures calculated above, perhaps as much as three or four times these amounts. Unfortunately no FTE estimates are yet available for the Mexican institutions.[44]

However, only the relative difference between the public and private ratios is of concern here, and the 2.3 point differential in the ratios above actually understates the amount of professors' time which is available to the students at the private universities. Table 4-9 gives the distribution of professors by time between public and private institutions.

TABLE 4-9

DISTRIBUTION OF PROFESSORS BY TYPE OF CONTRACT,
PUBLIC AND PRIVATE UNIVERSITIES, 1970-71

| | No. of Professors | | | |
| | Public | | Private | |
Type of contract	Universities	%	Universities	%
Full-time	2099	8.3	658	12.4
Half-time	1301	5.1	279	5.2
Hourly	22026	86.6	4395	82.4
	25426*	100.0	5332*	100.0

* Note: These figures do not include teaching assistants and "other" non-classifiiable instructors.

Source: ANUIES, *La Enseñanza Superior en México, 1971*, pp. 260ff.

Both private and public universities rely heavily on hourly instructors, to the extent of over 80 percent of their teaching members. At the level of half-time instructors, both types are nearly equally staffed on a percentage basis. But the private institutions have, percentage-wise, half again as many full-time instructors as the public institutions do. Thus an FTE calculation of students per teacher would show a much larger difference between public and private institutions.

Apparently, this trend toward full-time faculty is part of a conscious effort among many of the private universities to provide more student-teacher contact and to professionalize teaching careers at their institutions, as well as to attract and hold on to quality professorial resources.

At the Autonomous University of Guadalajara, for example, from 1966-1972 the number of full-time professors increased sharply from eighteen percent to 65 percent of the total faculty. This represents the largest growth of full-time faculty among the eight universities which reported this datum to the author, and a phenomenon unmatched by any of the universities interviewed. Monterrey Technological Institute also relies relatively heavily on full-time professors. About forty percent of their faculty is full-time, over half if only professional and graduate programs are considered.

It does not necessarily follow that more full-time professors means in and of itself better educational programs. Of critical importance, of course, is what these professors do in their working time, and how much the environment contributes to their productivity. Nevertheless, in general, it is a fact that the private institutions find themselves better staffed, with more total professors per student and with more of those professors employed on a full-time basis.

If it is true that there are more professors and more full-time professors at the private institutions, then the professorial wage bill should also show a higher percentage of per-student expenditures among private universities. The ANUIES data bear out this conclusion. If the 1970-71 data on expenditures for teachers' salaries are separated into public and private sectors, and each amount is divided by the number of students attending the reporting universities in each sector, the private universities spend about $172 per student on faculty, and the public institutions spend about $121 per student.[45] That is, of the $83 per student difference established earlier in this chapter between private and public schools on total expenditure per student, $51 or about sixty percent can be said to be spent on more or better faculty inputs. Thus it may be hypothesized that a large portion of the difference in total student costs between public and private universities lies in the cost of human resources employed. This result is consistent with the discussion contained earlier in this section.

In sum, the purpose of this section has not been to establish private universities as "better" than public ones. Indeed, on the basis of aggregate expenditure data this simply cannot and should not be done. What can be said, however, is that the private universities tend to spend more per student than the public ones. These funds go principally into the market place for teachers, and there they buy more and higher-priced resources. Thus it can be hypothesized that at least part of the preference for private universities and their graduates is understandable on economic grounds in terms of resource allocation. Other non-economic variables must be important, to be sure, and an attempt should be made to identify these on an institution-by-institution basis.

Conclusion

This chapter continues an analysis begun in Chapter Three with regard to differences between public and private sectors of Mexican higher education. The two sectors are significantly different, not only in size, but also in terms of structure and funding, recent growth trends and response to national goals, and in terms of quality considerations. This difference in quality is translatable into an economic framework in terms of differences in expenditure levels between the two sectors. The private sector is far more important to higher education than its size would indicate. In the context of this importance, the following chapter will relate this sector to the fulfillment of the future needs of Mexican higher education.

REFERENCES:

1   This chapter will also make use of data contained in Asociación Nacional de Universidades e Institutos de Enseñanza Superior, *La Enseñanza Superior en México*, various years.

2   *La Ley Orgánica de la UNAM* of 1944 in Carlos Alvear Acevedo, *La Educación y la Ley*, 1963, p. 247ff. The degree of autonomy enjoyed by the UNAM, at least legally, is unknown in the U. S. public universities. In return for the large appropriations made by the public sector (close to 100 million dollars in 1970-71), the Federal government has virtually no direct control over UNAM policies. However, the government does exercise considerable indirect influence.

3 The "free" part of the "compulsory, secular, and free" motto (see Chapter Two) has been applied to public higher education in Mexico as well. For example, tuition in UNAM currently is $16 per year. In 1970-71 tuitions and fees amounted to only about six percent of total income of the university. Donations accounted for less than one percent.

4 Many kinds of relationships are possible between government and university in Mexico. For more on these relationships for the provincial public universities, see Richard G. King, *The Provincial Universities of Mexico*, 1971, pp. 23-25.

5 The universities may be incorporated either as *asociaciones civiles (A.C.)*, non-profit legal entities, or as *sociedades civiles* or *sociedades anónimas* (S.C. or S.A.), which are organizations for profit. (There are some legal differences between S.C.'s and S.A.'s in the treatment of "profits", but these are ignored here.) While the great majority of universities are A.C.'s, a few are propietary, and two of these were included in the institutions of the study sample.

6 A current and complete list of degree granting universities in Mexico can be found in the ANUIES directory, published annually (ANUIES, *Directorio Nacional de Instituciones de Educación Superior*, year).

7 The Ford Foundation has been a major contributor to El Colegio. See Chapter Five.

8 Asociación Nacional de Universidades e Institutos de Enseñanza Superior, *La Obra Educativa del Régimen del Presidente López Mateos (1959-64), IV. La Educación Superior*, 1964, Table 3.

9 Meanwhile, enrollments in private provincial colleges did increase rapidly as well, somewhat more than doubling (3200 to 6700) over the period, a growth rate of about sixteen percent per year on an average.

10 See footnote fourteen, Chapter Three.

11 This growth of public *prepas* is understated because of the "loss" in 1968-69 of some 6,000 students in the *prepas* of the Universidad Veracruzana. By state government decree, these *preparatorias* were separated from the University's administrative cognizance.

12 The Colegio de México, nominally private, is excluded from this number for reasons discussed above. The rest of the private universities are considered private on the basis of funding. Further justification for the use of this variable as the determining one between public and private institutions will be offered in Chapter Five.

13 Some of these universities have enlarged enrollments because of *medio profesional* programs or *secundarias*, but the figures given reflect enrollments as previously defined.

14 See Charles Nash Myers, *Education and National Development in Mexico*, 1965, pp. 104-105:

A few highly capable students do receive a great deal of attention and are often carefully groomed by part-time professors for graduate work abroad . . . The rest of the students, however, receive relatively little attention, and some are motivated to complete their studies more by the prestige of the degree than by interest in the education it reflects. The individual student is very much on his own; the quality of his education depends to a high degree on his own ability and the effort he alone expends to develop it. It is for this reason that employers regard the National University in particular as the source of both the best and the worst graduates in the Republic.

15 In conjunction with the Centro de Investigaciones Económicas y de Negocios (Business and Economics Research Center) of the Autonomous University of Guadalajara.

16 The ten universities were:
1. UNAM (public)
2. Iberoamerican University (private)
3. University of Michoacán (public)
4. Autonomous University of Guadalajara (private)
5. Monterrey Technological Institute (private)
6. University of Nuevo León (public)
7. University of Guadalajara (public)
8. Autonomous Technological Institute of Mexico (private)
9. National Polytechnical Institute (public)
10. University of Veracruz (public)

17 Similar results were reported in 1968 by Cyrus Gibson. In a study conducted among executives of 300 firms in Mexico City, Guadalajara, and Monterrey, Gibson found a preference across fields for UNAM, National Polytechnic, and the Monterrey Technological. The Iberoamerican University was mentioned less often. However, when salaries for new managerial hires were investigated, the Iberoamerican graduates were reported to receive the highest average salaries, followed by Monterrey Technological, and then by the UNAM and IPN. See Cyrus F. Gibson, "The Development of Managers in Mexico — Report of a Survey" Mimeographed, Ford Foundation Study, January 1968. (Published in Spanish as "La Preparación de Gerentes en México," *Contabilidad y Administración*, No. 47, June 1968, pp. 5-30.)

18 Richard King, *op. cit.*, p. 22.

19 The nine universities in King's sample were: University of Guadalajara, University of Nuevo León, Autonomous University of San Luis Potosí, University of Sonora, University of Veracruz, University of Guanajuato, Autonomous University of the State of México, University of Michoacán, and the Monterrey Technological Institute (the lone private institution).

20 Richard King, *op. cit.*, p. 124.

21 For a discussion of such an organization with respect to a particular institution, the Iberoamerican University, see Francisco Migoya, "Universidad Iberoamericana, Mexico: The Ongoing Reform" in W. Roy Niblett and R. Freeman Butts, eds., *Universities Facing the Future*, 1972, pp. 137ff.

22 R. King, *op. cit.*, p. 124-5.

23 *Ibid.*, p. 124.

24 George R. Waggoner, "Problems in the Professionalization of the University Teaching Career in Central America, *Journal of Inter-American Studies,* Apr. 1968, *passim.*

25 R. King, *op. cit.,* p. 125.

26 This chapter was written by one of King's collaborators, Alfonso Rangel Guerra, Secretary General of ANUIES.

27 All of the deans who responded from Monterrey Technological Institute indicated that one or more kinds of incentives for research existed as a matter of regular university policy.

28 As an aside, it is interesting to note that notwithstanding the lack of incentives for research, over fifty of the some 275 public university professors reported publishing at least one journal article in the preceeding five years.

29 Not reporting either incomes or expenditures were La Salle University and the School of Banking and Commerce. El Colegio de México is not included in the private data.

30 Seventeen universities did not report. The largest of these contained 1070 students.

31 The Carnegie Commission on Higher Education, *The Capitol and the Campus,* 1971, p. 66. See also Joseph Froomkin, *Aspirations, Enrollments, and Resources,* 1970, p. 42, who reports that per-student expenditures in private universities are, as a rule, higher than those in public ones, with the exception of Catholic liberal arts colleges, (which, of course, receive considerable subsidies from religious orders who teach and administer at lower cost).

32 See Carnegie Commission, *op. cit.,* pp. 67-69.

33 The Mexican emphasis on free education, even at higher levels, has already been commented upon.

34 ANUIES approaches its bookkeeping differently than do most U.S. institutions. Expenditures are divided into: 1. Salaries and fees (subtitles: administrative, teaching, technical, and research personnel); 2. Cultural activities and scholarships ("Difusion Cultural"); 3. Capital expenditures (construction, equipment purchase, maintenance); 4. Other (in some cases "other" turns out to be the most important expenditure item!) For a description of U.S. practice see: Emerson Henke, *Accounting for Non-Profit Organizations,* 1966, pp. 85ff. and John D. Millett, *Financing Current Operations of American Higher Education,* 1972, *passim.*

35 A few larger universities, particularly public ones, did not break out their expenditures according to the ANUIES format, so they are not included in this analysis. Among these: IPN, Universities of Nuevo León, Veracruz, Coahuila, and the Valley of Mexico.

36 Five other private institutions of the study sample reported scholarships in various years that added from $7 to $31 to per-student costs.

37 In the U.S. in 1970, the number of graduate students amounted to about twelve percent of the total student attendance in universities.

38 University budgeting is almost never on a functional basis in Mexico and planned program budgeting is as yet all but untried. As Richard King puts it: "Budgeting is considered more an administrative necessity than a process of communication and a potential mechanism for ordering priorities among middle—and long-range programs." *Op. cit.*, p. 126.)

39 Simple correlations between enrollment size and per-student expenditures yields $r^2 = .35$ for public universities and $r^2 = .12$ for private institutions, indicating that about 35 percent of the variance in per-student costs among public universities can be associated with differences in size (inverse relationship, size up, costs down), but only 12 percent of the variance is likewise explainable among private universities (and in the opposite direction).

40 California and Western Conference, *Cost and Statistical Study for the Year 1954-55*, 1956, *passim*.

41 R. N. Calkins, in an analysis of cost data among 145 private liberal arts colleges in the U.S. indicates that the following variables are of prime importance in determining cost structures: level of faculty salaries, size of enrollment, curricular emphasis, and number of courses offered, in that order. *(The Unit Costs of Programs in Higher Education*, 1963.)

42 In the ANUIES format, included here are salaries for personnel in "teaching, research, and other related activities."

43 See Rudolph Atcon, *The Latin American University*, 1966, for a view of the traditional Latin American professor. Charles N. Myers *(Education and National Development in Mexico, 1967)*, presents the pros and cons of the part-time professor, the pros being in terms of cost savings for the country in her educational effort and the cons in terms of lack of professionalization of the teaching career. Richard King, *op. cit.*, also has some interesting comments on the preparation and performance of the part-time provincial professors.

44 By contrast, in the U.S., fully two thirds of the instructors in institutions of higher education teach full time. Calculating non-adjusted student/teacher ratios for the U.S., the figure is about 14.5/1. Using FTE professors, the ratio is over 18/1. Data for 1970; see Academic Media, *Standard Education Almanac, 1972*, pp. 144ff.

45 In 1970-71, 38 of the 78 public institutions and 29 of the 47 private universities reported expenditures according to the ANUIES format. A few larger public institutions, notably UNAM and IPN, whose per-student expenditures are above average, are not included. Therefore the difference between public and private universities in professorial salaries is slightly overstated. For example, if UNAM figures for 1968-69, the last year the ANUIES format was used, are included, average public per-student expenditures are $133, $12 more than the figure given here.

V : THE OUTLOOK FOR PRIVATE HIGHER EDUCATION

THE LAST CHAPTER INCLUDED A SURVEY of some details of the growth trends in higher education in Mexico in recent years. It will be useful here to review some of the overall tendencies of demographic growth in the country in order to project some of the likely trends in the demand for higher education.

Growth Trends

Mexico nearly doubled its population between 1950 and 1970. In fact, average annual population growth between 1960 and 1970 was somewhat faster (3.5 percent) than in the preceding decade (3.1 percent). The implications of this continual "baby boom" on the need for educational facilities and infrastructure in general are obvious and will put further pressure on public budgets.

From 1960-1970 the amount assigned to education in the Federal budget increased 360 percent, and the percentage of the total budget assigned to education went up from 9.7 percent to 14.2 percent.[1]

With regard to the demand for higher education, the rapid population growth from 1950 to date has delivered large numbers of new people into the fifteen-to-29-year-age group. From 1950-1960 this group increased from 7.3 million to about nine million, a change of some 23 percent. By 1970 the age group had increased to 12.4 million, or 38 percent over 1960.[2]

With these kinds of forces in motion the very large increases in university enrollments that were described in the last chapter — a 12.6 percent rate of growth in total university *prepas*, professional, and graduate schools from 1967-1971 — are to be expected. In 1960 there were 122 thousand students in the ANUIES-associated universities, *prepas* and above.[3] This amounts to about 1.4 percent[4] of the fifteen-to-29-year age groups of the 1960 census. In 1970 the number of students had risen to about 377 thousand,[5] or about 3.1 percent of the fifteen-to-29-year age groups. This is still a small percentage compared with countries such as the U.S. (53 percent) or even Chile

(18 percent.) (See Chapter Two.) During the next ten years both population trends and the needs of a growing economy will put further demands on Mexican universities, as the following projections indicate.

Raúl Benítez Zenteno has estimated Mexican population growth to 1985.[6] Using a constant fertility rate until 1965, declining linearly thereafter until 1985, he came within a million persons of predicting correctly the census estimates for 1960 and for 1970. Under his assumptions, Benítez' calculations show the rate of growth of the population falling off after 1965, and the number of children in the zero-to-four-year-age group dropping absolutely by 1975. But this downward effect does not reach up to the fifteen-to-nineteen (or older) age groups until after 1985, so that the college-age population continues to grow at least for the next decade. Latest estimates show population still growing at rates above 3.5 percent, so this growth may continue even longer than Benítez has projected. In any case, for 1980, Benítez' projection for the fifteen-to-29-year age group is about 18.2 million, which adds fifty percent to the potential college-demand group over the 1970 figures.

In addition, one should count on an increased percentage of this population demanding places in the nation's universities. If about three percent of the fifteen-to-29-year group was attending universities in 1970, this figure might easily be as high as five or six percent in 1980.[7] This would put one million or more students into the nation's universities by 1980, more than doubling the number that were attending in 1970. This kind of prediction may even be conservative given the average annual growth rate of the later part of the 1960's (1967-1971) which, if continued, would deliver to the university system some 1.5 million prospective students desiring enrollment by 1980. Expansion of this nature will severely tax the resources and the facilities of the already-overcrowded larger public universities, on the one hand, and, on the other, it could possibly mean a larger role for the private universities as they take up the load that the public universities are hard pressed to handle.

In the recent growth decade of U.S. higher education, 1960 to

1970, school enrollment of the twenty-to-24-year age group jumped from 13.1 to 21.5 percent, resulting in college enrollment across the nation that a bit more than doubled.[8] The accommodation of these students in U.S. universities was not accomplished without some difficulty, and no university began the period with the kind of overcrowding that exists today at the large Mexican public institutions, or stronger political pressures in favor of expanded educational opportunities than exist in Mexico.[9]

Implications of Growth: Costs

In terms of student costs, what will this increased enrollment bring as a national education bill by 1980? This can be tentatively estimated on the basis of recent growth in expenditures. The incomes[10] of ANUIES member universities increased 4.4 times from 1960 to 1970. Total students in these institutions in the meantime went up about 2.1 times. Thus per-student expenditures overall have more than doubled over the decade. Removing inflation from this increase,[11] expenditures have risen about 2.5 times, indicating some real growth in per-student expenditures during the period. Per-student costs have grown in the private universities as well. Among six private universities which reported this datum to the author, five had increased per-student costs from 1968 to 1972.[12] Among the five which experienced increases, these averaged 69 percent over the four years alone, a real growth of approximately fifty percent. Including the atypical university which found its per-student costs falling over the period, the average change in costs was about fifty-three percent.

The reasons for higher real costs, according to several of the university officials interviewed, are efforts to raise the quality of educational programs, and importantly, growing labor costs, particularly for instructors. Overall in Mexico, university labor costs have risen significantly during the 1960's from $3.4 million U.S. in 1960 to $37 million in 1969. The average yearly salary per employee has increased over the same period from $731 to $1,532, an increase of over 100 percent.[13] Mexico is often portrayed as a country of relatively cheap labor, but this impression has little validity in the higher-level technical and professional realms. In these areas, there is a large demand for highly qualified and trained personnel, who thus draw premium salaries within Mexico. The gap between the salaries of skilled and unskilled labor is considerably broader in Mexico than in the United States, and it may be this that makes Mexican labor look cheap to the outsider. But at the same time, many Mexican firms, universities included, find that their largest resource bill is for skilled labor.

Projecting per-student costs, basing the projections on the trends above, an increase exceeding the average inflation rate by several points can confidently be predicted for the 1970's. Combining this with a foreseeable doubling of the university population yields a growth of the total university education bill in the present decade that will approximate or exceed the kind of growth that took place in higher education in the United States in the 1960's. In this decade, U.S. university enrollment almost exactly doubled, and per-student expenditures increased at a rate about three points higher than the average inflation rate for the period.[14] Of course, Mexican university growth may be qualitatively nothing like U.S. university expansion because of considerations such as Mexico City polarization, the lack of a junior college movement and arts and sciences training, and a growing emphasis on subprofessional and technical training in Mexico, among other things. But the U.S. model may serve as a guide to the size of resource allocation effort that is needed, and in particular, to the necessity for an increase in awareness of the "publicness" of the private universities as they take up the quantitative and qualitative overload on the public universities.

For there could be two main effects of this large-scale expansion of Mexican higher education and its costs over the present decade. One might be a tendency toward increased public sector budgetary emphasis from the primary and secondary schools (particularly primary) to higher levels of education. This would have some important public finance implications that will be discussed later in this chapter. It would be a troublesome problem given the necessity of bringing primary schooling to large and increasing numbers of the rural uneducated. The second effect, already referred to, would be the tendency for private universities to play a more public role in the education of Mexico's future professionals, opening their doors to the nation's young people in larger measure than private universities have done in the U.S. in the last decades.[15] This would be somewhat problematic, given the setting of Mexican private education, as will be seen presently; but it will clearly be important under the needed expansion as projected above.

If one accepts these implications of future growth, particularly the second, it is important to explore the question of flexibility that the private universities may have for assuming an increasing pubilc role. In particular, what means are at the disposal of the private universities for substantially increasing their enrollments and incurring the higher per-student expenditures that accompany quality improvement and the increasing costs of qualified labor input? It will be convenient to discuss these under the four principal potential sources of funds, namely, tuitions, government support, gifts and endowments, and auxiliary enterprises.

Tuitions

Private universities in Mexico rely very heavily on tuitions and fees for income. In the ANUIES data for 1970-71, fifteen of the thirty private institutions reporting their incomes received one hundred percent of that income from tuitions and fees. The remaining fifteen institutions received an average of 76 percent of their total income from tuitions and fees. These figures may overstate the case somewhat since double-entry balance between incomes and expenditures is not adhered to in the ANUIES data, and twelve of the fifteen institutions reported expenditures which were more than their incomes. These deficits must be covered somehow, and it is reasonable to presume that the funds usually come from grants by private individuals or firms who are interested in these universities.

A better indicator of this tendency to reliance on tuitions can be found in the data reported to the author by seven[16] of the more important private institutions. Of these, two reported one hundred percent dependence on tuitions (one is a proprietary institution), and the others received other sources of support in varying amounts. The average percentage reliance on tuitions for all seven of the institutions was about 79 percent. In general then, a fair estimate would be that, among the important private institutions, tuitions count for approximately seventy-five to eighty percent of all incomes. By U.S. standards, of course, this figure is very high. William G. Bowen reports that the average percentage of incomes received in tuitions by all the U.S. private universities was, in 1963-1964, only about 35 percent of total incomes.[17] For some of the larger, more prestigious institutions the average was even less. This percentage has been dropping over the last few decades,[18] Bowen points out, but even as early as the twenties it was only about fifty percent, far below the current level in Mexico.

How has the level of tuitions been moving among the private universities in Mexico? The data considered here is limited to a series over the four-year-period 1968 through 1972 for nine of the largest private institutions.[19] The average increase for the nine universities was 53 percent over the four-year period, or an average annual rate of growth of 11.2 percent. This rate of increase is considerably above that of the U.S. private universities included in Bowen's study, which, since about 1958, had shown tuition increases averaging about eight percent per annum. The rate does correspond to the average increase in per-student costs among the Mexican private universities which was about 53 to 69 percent over the four years, or an average annual growth rate of between 11.2 and 14.0 percent.

Comparing the growth in costs with the growth in tuitions it is seen that for most universities the former has been leading changes in fee incomes by nearly three percentage points. However, including in the average cost calculations the atypical university whose per-student costs were declining over the recent period, the growth in costs then averages about the same as the growth in tuition earnings. These findings generally correspond to those of Bowen for U.S. private universities in the post-war period. (His figures are about eight percent for tuitions and about 7.5 percent for per-student costs.) In reality, given the limited amount of data available for the Mexican private institutions the best hypothesis seems to be that costs and fee incomes have risen at about a par in the last few years although a substantial number of universities have been having difficulties in keeping abreast of rising costs.

Donations and Gifts, Endowments.

In the ANUIES income data for 1970-71, the thirty reporting private universities had only about one-and-a-half million dollars of donations among them, and eighteen of the thirty reported no gifts whatsoever. Of the total income received by the private institutions, about seven percent came from donations. Again the amount is probably understated because of the occurrence of non-accounted-for deficits. In the author's data from the six private universities which reported incomes from 1968 to 1972, two had no income outside tuitions, and the average for all six was about fourteen percent of budget receipts received in the form of gifts and grants. Thus it might appear that private philanthropic assistance for the major private universities is about on a par with that of the U.S., where gifts and grants for all private universities was about twelve percent of incomes in 1963-1964.[20] However, there is a problem in the extension of that generalization because there are very few "major" private universities in Mexico and there are large differences among their individual data. Averages are thus misleading. Another point to be noted is that among the "major" universities there are a few which are run for profit.[21] Thus, donations are not a part of their income picture and this makes for a lower overall average than would otherwise be the case under pure non-profit conditions.[22]

In general, voluntary giving is not as established a part of the overall Mexican context of higher education as it is in the United States. This is particularly true among the public universities, which receive almost no support in terms of private gifts and grants from firms or individuals, either from sources internal to the country or external to it. In fact, of the 58 public universities who reported their incomes to ANUIES in 1970-71, only fifteen cited any income at all from gifts and grants, and those amounts varied from less than one to about four percent of receipts.[23]

By contrast, in the U.S. among the public universities, voluntary support amounted to about 4.4 percent of total educational and general expenditures in 1970-1971. For some of the biggest receivers of private support, such as the University of California system and the University of Michigan, the percentage was over ten percent.[24]

One important difference in the Mexican context of gift-giving is that there are few private philanthropic foundations in Mexico, and none approaching the size of such U.S. organizations as Ford, Rockefeller, and Danforth, for example. In a list prepared by Ann Stromberg in 1966, there were a total of 29 Mexican foundations, none of whose capital assets exceeded two million dollars, and only nine of which operated fairly broadly in the field of education. These nine foundations distributed a total of only some 600 thousand dollars in 1966, not a very large quantity even by Mexican standards.[25]

In addition, some of the large American and other foreign foundations do make grants available to Mexican universities. For example, over the four years from 1969 through 1972, Monterrey Technological Institute received over a million dollars from Ford, Rockefeller, and Lurgi and Ferrostal, A.G. An especially noteworthy case has been that of El Colegio de México. From 1963 to 1973 the Ford Foundation contributed 1.3 million dollars to establish and support the Colegio's Center for Economic and Demographic Studies. This was followed in 1973 by an endowment grant of $2 million from the Foundation. Apart from Monterrey Technological and El Colegio, however, foundation assistance does not contribute large amounts to university budgets, and on balance the foundation has not been a significant force in higher education in Mexico.

There has developed in Mexico a substitute for the lack of philanthropy among the major private universities. This phenomenon has coincided with the organization of the two archetypal private universities for which gift support is a major source of current revenue. A sketch of the operations of these universities will help explain the Mexican application of the role of philanthropy among the major private universities. The two institutions are the Monterrey Techno-logical Institute (ITESM) and the Autonomous Technological In-stitute of Mexico (Instituto Tecnológico Autónomo de México — ITAM). Both were founded by groups of executives of large firms as non-profit educational ventures, the first in Monterrey and the second in Mexico City. Their purpose, from the founders' point of view, was to produce technicians and administrators as human re-source inputs for the firms in those two industrial cities. Probably due to the strength of their idea and the political force of the industri-alists behind it, both universities achieved autonomy from the gov-ernment in the fullest sense, not only financial, but also in that they have full degree-granting power without the necessity of incorpo-rating their studies in a state or federal institution. They are *"uni-versidades libres,"* "free universities."

Both these institutions continue to rely heavily on their parent "foundations" for financial (and moral) support. In the case of ITESM, the annual subsidy has averaged about 800 thousand dollars from 1969 to 1972. Although the amount of the subsidy has varied each year, the percentage it represents of the total budget has de-creased over the four-year period with the brunt of expenditures being increasingly covered by tuition and fees. In addition, the "foundation" each year contributes to the "fixed assets" of the uni-versity, in the form of a building fund. Sums allocated to this fund over the four years cited have amounted to nearly two million dollars.

With regard to the ITAM the participation of the *"patronato,"* or the parent foundation, is somewhat greater, amounting to as much as fifty percent of current receipts. Plans for the future are that tu-itions cover about seventy percent of expenditures with external funds from the *patronato* and elsewhere, covering the remainder. ITAM is fortunate to count among its graduates a fairly large num-ber of managers and officials of important firms in Mexico, and they keep alive the private business interest in the university that was res-ponsible for its founding.

There are other private universities that likewise enjoy to some extent the participation of private firms. Universidad Iberoamericana, for example, some years after its founding, gained the support of a group of Mexico City industrialists. This group has been responsible for the construction of several important buildings for the University. The Autonomous University of Guadalajara (Universidad Autónoma de Guadalajara — UAG) although not formed primarily to produce professionals for Guadalajara's firms, still does benefit from contributions from these firms in small measure, particularly from the world's largest tequila producer, the Sauza Company. Sauza recently contributed funds for the building of a computer center on the UAG campus. However, total contributions to current funds in the last two or three years have amounted to only about two percent or so of the budget. Another Guadalajara university, the Western Technological Institute of Higher Studies, regularly receives donations from private firms. These amounted to 27 percent of its budget in 1970-71. A few other newer private institutions, such as the Instituto Panamericano de Humanidades (IPH) in Mexico City and the Centro de Enseñanza Técnica y Superior in Mexicali also have backing that contributes substantial amounts (seventy percent or more in the case of IPH) to current budgets.

Very close to gifts in the Mexican context, as can be seen above in the discussion of ITESM and ITAM, are endowments, which do not really exist as a thing apart among the Mexican universities. In the ANUIES data only three or four institutions show income that could be considered as coming from endowments, and these incomes are very small parts (one percent or so) of total receipts. Endowments, such as they are, tend to be associated with regular gifts and with moral and political support rather than with funds established to yield income. At the ITESM and the ITAM, for example, the *patronato* has been very important to the development of the institutions even though no formal endowment has been established. At the UAG and the Womens' University, the founders continue to make donations to the university and a few serve without salary, forming at least a short-run endowment. The fact is that the development boom that produced great personal wealth in the United States at the turn of the century, and which left a base for private philanthropy, only began in Mexico very recently. There are indications that some of this wealth is finding its way into the universities, but that effort is yet in its infancy. In the future it could well become an expanding component in private university income.

Government Grants

As was mentioned in Chapter Four, the public universities subsist almost totally on government funds, either state or federal. Examining the aggregate figures of public university incomes,[26] seventy to 75 percent of total funds assigned to these incomes come from federal sources, about fifteen to twenty percent more from state subsidies, and the rest from "own university funds," i.e., tuitions, gifts, etc. These aggregate figures are somewhat deceiving because the two big federal universities which receive only federal funds, the UNAM and the National Polytechnic, weigh heavily in the figures. These two universities received fully 90 percent of the total federal subsidy in 1970-71, leaving relatively little for other public institutions. If these two are removed from the accounting, quite a different picture emerges: federal funds count for nearly thirty percent of the total, state funds count over a half, and "own funds" make up the rest. The details of this distribution are spelled out in Table 5-1, which gives the amounts of funds and their relative percentages for 1960 and 1970.

The private universities, however, receive almost no government aid, either state or federal. Of the 30 private universities who reported incomes to ANUIES in 1970-71, only one received any outright government grant, Monterrey Technological Institute. From the author's knowledge of the other important universities which did not report, it can confidently be said that the Institute is unique in this regard.[27] In fact, this practice is so rare that one can make a clear distinction between public and private universities on this basis. The dichotomy between public and private sector education in this respect is pronounced and well-defined; the public purse does not support private education and, vice-versa, the private sector does not

TABLE 5-1

SOURCES OF FUNDS TO ANUIES PUBLIC MEMBER UNIVERSITIES
1960 and 1970

(U.S. thousands of dollars)

Year	Federal subsidies	%	State subsidies	%	Own funds	%	Total funds	%
1960	$20,829	73	$ 5,187	18	$ 2,337	8	$ 28,353	100
1970	90,532	73	19,950	16	13,046	10	123,528	100

WITHOUT UNAM & IPN

Year	Federal subsidies	%	State subsidies	%	Own funds	%	Total funds	%
1960	$ 2,445	29	$ 5,187	61	867	10	$ 8,499	100
1970	10,376	27	19,950	52	7,715	20	38,041	100

UNAM

Year	Federal subsidies	%	State subsidies	%	Own funds	%	Total funds	%
1960	$10,346	88	-----------	----	$ 1,470	12	$ 11,816	100
1970	45,186	89	-----------	----	5,331	11	50,517	100

IPN

Year	Federal subsidies	%	State subsidies	%	Own funds	%	Total funds	%
1960	$ 8,038	100	-----------	----	-----------	----	$ 8,038	100
1970	34,970	100	-----------	----	-----------	----	34,970	100

Source: ANUIES, *La Enseñanza Superior en México, 1966 and 1970, passim.*

contribute to the public university. This dichotomy stems from a tradition that will be examined presently.

A closer look at the unique case of Monterrey Technological Institute will be worthwhile. In the three years 1969 to 1971 inclusively, the federal government has subsidized the Institute with two million pesos ($160,000 U.S.) of grants each year. In 1972 the subsidy was higher, almost three million pesos. In addition, the government pays the tuition of a number of students; in 1972 this sum amounted to some 27 thousand dollars. Two million pesos was, however, only three percent of the 1969 budget, and the 1972 subsidy of 2.9 million was still only about three percent of expenditures. Nevertheless, even though this quantity may be low by U.S. standards (Bowen reports that government grants and contracts amounted to nearly *half* of the Chicago-Princeton-Vanderbilt average educational and general income),[28] by Mexican standards it is unique. Perhaps it is, moreover, a pilot effort with respect to future public support of private universities in Mexico.

The reason for the lack of public funds channeled into private universities can be understood in the light of the history of Mexican education outlined in Chapter Two. For all of the colonial period, and for many years afterward, private education, virtually the only education, was non-secular and ecclesiastical. Except for early attempts by Fray Pedro de Gante, Don Vasco de Quiroga, and a few others to bring learning to the Indians and *mestizos,* education was largely for the privileged who could afford to pay for it. Not that this elitism was unique to Mexico; it has existed all over Latin America in various degrees. But the thrust of the public education movement in Mexico particularly since the Revolution of this century has been to open up education to the masses of Mexicans who could not afford to pay for it. Thus result the low tuitions among the state institutions and the acceptance by the government of its role as the national educator.

In addition, another thread of Mexican history which must be followed through is the anticlericalism which resulted in the War of Reform (1858-1861) and in a long history of conflict between church and state in Mexico.[29] The reasons for this conflict are now buried in Mexican history and turn about the political and economic power of the Church in the 19th Century. Also involved was the alliance between the Church and the conservative forces which backed the French Intervention and opposed Juárez and his liberals. But anticlericalism was written into the liberal constitutions of 1857 and those that followed, and is still an important force in Mexico today. It is so important, in fact, that there are officially still no Church-run schools in the country. Some universities such as the Iberoamerican, the Western Technological Institute, La Salle, Anáhuac, and a few others have Church connections, or more correctly, religious order connections. But officially they are not owned by the Church or the order, although they may enjoy the subsidy of the religious who teach and/or administer.[30]

What has all this to do with the non-church private universities? First, in the 19th Century liberal context, "private" meant "church-owned" and the reaction against private education became embedded in the liberal tradition. Moreover, Juárez believed that only in the hands of the state could education be liberalized and extended to the masses. If tuitions had to be paid, in a private-sector context, education would continue to be elitist. It is curious that whereas liberalism embraced the free market in Europe and in North America, in Mexico the market was rejected, at least with respect to education. Finally, Mexico went through a period of toying with state socialism in the 1930's. The constitution was amended under Article 3 to give the State the sole authority to impart primary, secondary, and normal schooling. This was the final version; a previous version stated that *all* levels of education were to be "socialist in their orientation and tendencies."[31] The State would revoke, at its own discretion, the license of a school which did not follow these norms, and from the revocation there would be no recourse. President Calles issued what came to be called the "Cry of Guadalajara" and let it be known that education was not exclusively a function of the home and parents, but of the State since "The child . . . belongs to the community, to the people . . ."[32] So it was clear that private education at whatever level, religious and non-religious, was in trouble, and that all education was to be an affair closely prescribed by the State.

This radical socialist mood continued in Mexico until well into the 1940's when President Ávila Camacho began to soften the hard line and retreat somewhat from the extreme left position. Finally in 1946, the famous Article 3 of the Constitution was again rewritten, private education was reestablished subject to government supervision, and education in general was returned to the hands of the parents.

In this context, the youth and immaturity of the private universities, and the lack of empathy between the private universities and the State are understandable results.

Monterrey Technological Institute is indeed unique among private universities since public support of that institution goes against the history and tradition of the public-private education dichotomy. That the Institute has been successful is a reflection of the reputation acquired by the university and a measure of the amount of political influence that its backers have enjoyed.

Auxiliary Enterprises

In recent years in the United States, university ventures into the world of ordinary business has been one of the most talked-about developments in education reviews and popular journals. Probably the most famous, or notorious, case was that of Parsons College and its flamboyant president, Dr. Millard Roberts, who sought to convert a private university into a profitable operation and destroyed it in the process.[33] But there have been other examples of institutions which have tried to capture needed income through a variety of commercial activities, some of which involved education and research by-products, others which have taken the university out of its traditional role as transmitter of knowledge and promoter of research into widely varied ventures such as real estate and development projects, commercial buildings, and others. Indiana University, for example, has patents on the formula for a leading toothpaste which yield up to $100,000 per year in income. A more out-of-the-ordinary example is Knox College, a small Illinois liberal-arts institution, which has owned, among other things, a resort motel in Utah, orange groves in Florida, and a racetrack near Chicago. One of the largest and most successful of these university-as-entrepreneur endeavors has been the one carved out by Stanford University. This scheme has turned some 6,000 acres of prime California land into a revenue producer that contributes substantially to the university budget.

It will probably not be surprising that the Mexican universities have not yet come to use auxiliary enterprises as significant inputs into their budget receipts. Fewer than twenty of the 88 public and private universities which reported to ANUIES in 1970-71, listed receipts which could be considered as coming from these kind of sources. Among those that had such sources, the income received usually amounted to no more than three-to-five percent of total receipts.

One of the differences between the development of U.S. and Mexican universities in this context is that dormitories, a traditional source of enterprise income among U.S. institutions, never came to be built at Mexican universities. There are several reasons for this: one is that most Mexican universities have been municipal universities serving their own metropolitan areas. The concept of the out-of-state student, or the out-of-town student for that matter, is a relatively recent one in Mexico and one that has come about because of the overcrowding and non-availability of local universities as well as because of increased personal income.

Secondly, most universities do not have campuses in the U.S. sense on which to put student residences, or other revenue-raising activities. As a facet and probably as part of the cause of the career isolationism which was commented upon in the last Chapter, there is a physical isolation of the different disciplines in various building scattered throughout the city. The reason for this has been a straightforward economic one, lack of capital for construction, resulting in the use of converted buildings wherever they could be found, and the continued use of antiquated buildings long after their utility as educational facilities had been outgrown. Integrated campuses have been a goal of many universities as funds have become more available, but so far few have realized this goal.

One private university which has been the exception to the above rule, Monterrey Technological Institute, did plan for students from all over the Republic and built residences to house over one thousand of them. This investment has in recent years returned as much as 280 thousand dollars, about five percent of the Institute's total budget, and thus Monterrey Technological Institute ranks high among Mexican universities in the funds it receives from auxiliary enterprises. Others, such as the UAG, are beginning to explore this avenue of income in their educational planning. One of the UAG's very interesting projects will be presented in a later section.

Projecting Costs and Incomes

Earlier in this chapter it was estimated that per-student expenditures in public universities had approximately doubled from 1960 to 1970. Actually the figure was exactly double for the public member universities, the incomes and student enrollments of which increased at an annual rate of 16 percent and eight percent respectively. Thus the annual rate of growth of per-capita student expense was between seven and 7.5 percent. Subtracting out the average annual inflation rate of the 1960's, 3.5 percent, real growth was about three to four percent. In the smaller sample of six private universities, the average annual rate of increase of per-student costs was somewhat higher, 10.7 percent from 1968 to 1972, a real rate of increase of about five to six percent. The simplest method of projection of future costs is to extrapolate the past rate of growth, and this is considered a reasonable approach since the pressures that have pushed costs up in the last few years will continue into the next decade. Thus an increase of costs among the private universities at about five points above the average inflation rate is assumed for the 1970's. Estimates of future trends on the basis of limited data should be approached with great caution, but this kind of projection is consistent with continued efforts to increase the quality of the educational programs at the universities. There will be increased need for more highly trained professors, better libraries, more research, more graduate relative to undergraduate education, and other program improvements. The urgency of these improvements is being perceived by the private universities and this perception has been responsible for the cost increases of recent years.

It is possible that costs may rise even faster if overcrowding at the public universities forces up the rate of enrollment in the private schools. Enrollments of the private universities in general have increased at about a 11.5 percent rate over the end years of the 1960's. (See Table 4-1.) Among the six universities of the cost sample, however, the rate of growth, although it varied widely between the individual schools, averaged only about 4.5 percent a year during the most recent years. If these institutions were to take on a heavier load, it is probable that their costs would be driven up even faster, since economies of scale could likely be overreached. This kind of trend is impossible to establish with any kind of accuracy, but it may be said that the inflation-plus-five percent cost projection could be a conservative one.

The projection of incomes is, as Bowen has said, an extremely hazardous undertaking. Whereas forces producing changes in costs may operate in a fairly predictable manner, the factors affecting the components of income can vary in unforeseen ways. Tuitions, however, are probably the most predictable of incomes, so an attempt to forecast them for the private universities is made first.

Tuitions: Possibilities

As reported earlier, tuitions and fees have increased among nine of the major private universities at an average annual rate of slightly over eleven percent in recent years. This rapid rate of price increase is higher than that reported by Bowen for U.S. private institutions (about eight percent) and four to five points higher than other price movements in Mexico. The question becomes, can the private universities continue to increase tuitions at a rate of about eleven percent per year in the 1970's in order to match the expected increases in costs?

At the outset, it may be instructive to say that the universities feel keenly the possible price elasticity of tuition rates. When asked about increases, the respondents from several of the universities expressed concern over their ability to continue increases, and one was even somewhat defensive about the subject. All of the respondents did feel, however, that tuitions would have to be raised over time and that the limitations on doing so would restrict improvements that were necessary for the development of the institution.

From what has been written about the returns to education to the individual, one might be surprised at the concern expressed by the universities. Martin Carnoy[34] has shown that in urban Mexico the private internal rate of return to completion of university education is 35 percent or better and that it exceeds the return to any other level except completion of primary school. In fact, the private rate of return to college education in Mexico was found to be higher than for any other country in the Western hemisphere for which it had been studied, with the exception of Brazil.[35] That this kind of payoff would not be perceived by families who are sending their children to college in Mexico would be hard to conceive, but apparently university administrators think that educational costs weigh heavily in parents and students' decisions and that rate of return considerations notwithstanding, college attendance is fairly price-elastic.[36]

Why this should be so cannot be completely answered here. Conversations with university officials on this point in the sample institutions turned about several points: competition from other (private and public) universities, particularly in the case of the Mexico City institutions;[37] considerations of "fairness" for students from middle-class families who would have difficulty meeting higher fees; and other factors. One important factor was a consideration for the students already attending the institutions; some universities were particularly concerned about raising the tuitions of those students for fear of provoking the kind of difficulties so prevalent in the public institutions. One institution, the UAG, follows a practice which has only recently gained some acceptance in the United States, that of fixing a student's fee at first inscription, so that tuition increases apply to new students but not to ones already enrolled. This same university has also discovered some important inelasticities in a particular sector of its student body. For the last several years the UAG has been admitting in increasing numbers U.S. medical students who for one reason or another cannot find space in American medical schools. In 1974-75, there were some three thousand American students in the school, making UAG the largest "U.S." medical school in the world. In the last few years, tuition has been doubled for these students, to two thousand dollars per semester, and there is apparently still excess demand. No similar experiment has been conducted with the Mexican student component, however.

On balance it would appear that the private universities are clearly concerned that the tuition increases of recent years cannot be maintained indefinitely. They may be correct in their concern for two reasons. First, the private universities' tuitions have risen faster than other prices. In particular, the general price index[38] rose at an average of 6.8 percent from 1969 to 1973, and this represents an increase over past rates.[39] During the same period, the price increase for education and entertainment in general averaged about seven percent. Thus an eleven percent rate of growth of tuitions was relatively high.

Secondly, personal income projections by one of Mexico's foremost economists, Ifigenia G. de Navarrete, show a relative slowing down in the rate of personal income increase for higher level income earners.[40] Mrs. Navarrete suggests that Mexico is moving toward less wealth concentration in the 1970's and that, although real income for all income levels will increase, the lower and middle levels will rise at a faster rate than the higher levels. By "higher levels" she means those whose monthly incomes in 1963 averaged about eight thousand pesos in 1958 prices, precisely that level at which people could have begun to afford the expenses of a private university education for their children.

Perhaps Mrs. Navarrete also offers us a key to the apparent paradox offered by the Carnoy data. If the returns to college education are so high, how can it be that they are not perceived by the Mexican public? The answer may lie in part in the fact that relatively few people (ten percent in the Navarrete data), those in the upper-income level, can afford the capital outlay that it takes to reap the later return, and these few generally have the means and the knowledge to shop about for the best educational bargain.

It is not known how many private university students actually come from upper-income groups, but the writer, following the Navarrete data, suggests that ninety percent would not be too high an estimate. These families have the option of sending their children to several private universities and even to the U.S., although relatively few do the latter, at the undergraduate level.[41] At the provincial universities of the author's study sample, UAG and Monterrey Technological, half or more of the students come from out-of-state, mostly from Northern states, so these two universities are probably competing for many of the same students. At the Mexico City institutions, most of the students are from the Federal District, so the market is again fairly well defined.

In any case, high tuitions tend to limit the private university's market even more than it is already limited by the given income distribution.[42] This kind of thought process may be what is implicitly involved in tuition decisions among administrators.

The above pricing issue also puts the private universities squarely back into an elitist framework, which is another horn of the dilemma for them. Tuition increases obviously price some people out, mainly those from the growing middle class. So the question remains how much can tuitions grow at the "average" private university over the next few years? It is this writer's hypothesis that they grow no faster than the five to six percent-over-inflation rate of the last few years, and probably that they "should not" grow much faster than the price index for most goods. This kind of hypothesis is consistent with a "democratization" of the private universities, or an increase in their "publicness" as it was previously expressed.

If private universities find themselves limited with regard to price increases, as this hypothesis suggests, then where might funds come from in order to meet the higher costs that will necessarily be incurred in the effort to produce the quality education that the country needs?

One possibility might lie in student loans, particularly in a new type of loan which is gaining some attention in the United States, the "income-contingent" or "variable-term" tuition loan. This idea of a loan tied to future income was first proposed some thirty years ago by Milton Friedman and Simon Kuznets,[43] and in its current state of refinement offers many advantages for students over ordinary loan programs. Under this type of plan a student is able to borrow funds for education expenses at a variable interest rate; the student contracts only for a repayment rate, or the percentage of income to be paid each year, and the maximum repayment period beyond which he no longer need pay. The cost of the loan, or the interest rate, is determined later by the "payoff" of the student's education, i.e., his future income stream. The higher the income, the higher the repayment, up to a certain limit (e.g., 150 percent of principal plus a market rate of interest) beyond which no one pays. Low-income earners stand to have the cheapest loans, and many would receive partial forgiveness after the maximum payment period expires.[44] At least two private universities in the U.S., Yale and Duke Universities, have been experimenting with this kind of tuition loan, but the capital requirements of such a program are fairly high, depending upon market interest and payback parameters. Total debt outstanding for $1000 loaned might run as high as $1500-$1600.[45] These kinds of quirements, while possible for a Yale or a Duke, might be overly burdensome for most Mexican institutions while they are still very busy meeting capital requirements for program and facilities development. The idea of the income contingent loan has, however, been seriously discussed at at least one Mexican institution, the UAG.

It appears that a more viable possibility in the Mexican context would be a government-sponsored loan program along the lines of the income-contingent payback concept. Such program could be planned, under guidelines available in the literature, for zero long-run cost to the government. Or, given the high social rate of return to higher education,[46] the program might be combined with subsidies to lower-income students to make the loans even more attractive, although from the U.S. experience it is not clear that this latter is necessary.[47] Most importantly, the Federal government is in a much better position than are the universities to support the capital requirements of a loan program. Given the social return, the opportunity costs of such capital investment might well turn out to be negative.

Finally, if such a loan program could be made available to all students, public and private, then the government would avoid a tradition-jogging change of policy toward the private universities. Because students at private universities would presumably need larger loans than those attending public universities, more equal treatment would be given the former students vis-a-vis public subsidies, without necessarily reducing public expenditures elsewhere.

Both public and private vehicles exist for the channeling of student loans. The most important of these has been the National Council for Science and Technology (Consejo Nacional de Ciencia y Tecnología — CONACYT). Founded in 1970 to promote scientific and technical awareness and to encourage Mexican efforts in this area, CONACYT has in the first four years of its existence provided about 15 million dollars in loans/scholarships for some 5000 graduate and undergraduate students.[48] So far most of these grants have been for study abroad.

The Banco de México, the national bank, also provides unsecured credits to students at low interest rates.[49] From 1965 to 1974 some four million dollars have been loaned to 1200 students. Lastly, a private scholarship agency called Central de Becas (Center for Scholarships) was formed in 1968 by a group of Mexican firms. By the end of 1973, this non-profit organization had made over 900 grants totaling more than a million dollars. These agencies have broken much ground in providing funds for students, but much more remains to be done given the volume of students to be accomodated by Mexican universities in the next decades.

It is this writer's opinion that an income-contingent student loan program through any or all of these established conduits could be one of the most viable ways of meeting higher costs among Mexican public and private universities. Whether or not such a program could become operational would depend on the skill of university scholars and officials in presenting a case for these loans to policymakers and upon the satisfactory translation of the mechanics of the concept itself into the Mexican milieu.

Gifts, Grants, and Endowments: Possibilities

As was mentioned earlier in the Chapter, private universities in Mexico vary widely as to their ability to attract gift income to themselves. Among the six universities sampled, donations ranged from zero percent of their budgets (for two institutions, one proprietary), to about two percent for the UAG, eleven percent for the Ibero-american, twenty percent for Monterrey Technological, and fifty percent for ITAM. These latter universities have become very aware in recent years of the potential of gift-giving and currently carry on fund-raising efforts of various degrees of sophistication. One, the UAG, has published a guide to fund-raising techniques.[50]

Among the universities which have become involved in the search for gifts and grants, much emphasis has been on restricted funds, gifts used for special projects such as buildings or sports facilities. The ITESM has also received donations, notably from American foundations, earmarked for student aid. However, at some universities, at least, significant portions of general expenditures are covered by unrestricted funds; such was the case at ITESM and ITAM. The UAG, on the other hand, prides itself on never needing or asking for donations except for construction and for improvement of programs or facilities. In this way it attempts to preserve its autonomy from outside influences.

What does the future hold for these universities in their search for donations for current and investment purposes? Much will depend on the efforts of the universities themselves. Mexican tax laws are similar to those of the U.S. with regard to deductibility of gifts, so campaigns to alert the community to the needs of the institution and its value to the community and to the firms of the community can be fruitful. This is the tack that the UAG has been taking recently, and programs have been organized around public relations and relations with the private firm. In building its new campus, the UAG collected a million and a quarter dollars from firms and individuals interested in the university's progress. From 1968 through 1971 receipts were more modest, but still amounted to some two hundred thousand dollars. The ITESM and ITAM have similar programs, the latter recently receiving about a million-and-a-half dollar grant from an important national banking and credit group. It is to be stressed that the universities mentioned have systematized their fund-raising activities, somewhat along the lines of U.S. institutions. Without this kind of organization, still new to the Mexican universities, the lack of participation of the community in higher educaton will continue.[51]

In any case, it would appear that there is some flexibility with regard to the university's ability to participate in private philanthropy. Campaigns among alumni and among students' parents have yielded excellent results at the universities which have attempted to tap these sources. Although Mexican foundations may be limited in resources, some funds are available from this source,[52] and in addition, there may be some possibility that American foundations could turn more of their attention to Mexico, as in the case of the Ford and Rockefeller contributions cited earlier. Personal bequests have apparently not been of great importance. Perhaps a contributing factor here is the lack of any death or gift taxes in Mexico.[53] However, the possibilities of tapping this source of wealth are there.

One kind of bequest deserves special mention because of its application at two universities in the sample, namely, land bequests on the Stanford pattern both to provide the university with an appreciating long-term capital base and to give the donors a return in the form of enhanced land values around the site. In a developing urban area this can be an excellent technique for providing incentives to develop needed university facilities. More will be said about this particular kind of land bequest later since it coordinates with the concept of auxiliary enterprises that will be developed in a following section.

Government Grants; Possibilities

From the historical sketch above, it can be understood that the possibilities for most private universities to secure government grant assistance are fairly limited. This is especially true with respect to the so-called "confessional" universities, i.e., the sectarian universities, since their very existence is only reluctantly recognized by the State. These institutions with religious origins, e.g. Iberoamerican University, Western Technological Institute (ITESO), Anáhuac, La Salle and a few others, will have some difficulty in overcoming tradition and obtaining government support. Due to the difficult political

conditions surrounding the history and founding of the UAG, it will
also have problems similar to the sectarian universities, although
the UAG has never sought government assistance.

It must be noted here that all the universities that are A.C.'s or
non-profit organizations, enjoy income tax exemptions that are the
equivalent of government subsidies. Some further advances are being made along these lines; recently Iberoamericana received the
remission of half its property tax to the Federal District.

But for any kind of sizable transfer of funds from public to private sector higher education, such as that which occurs in the U.S.,
the outlook is rather bleak. The reason for this judgement is the
scale of government commitment to primary and secondary schooling. In addition, there is some lack of flexibility in the Mexican tax
system.

Earlier in this chapter it was mentioned that Mexico's federal education budget had more than quadrupled during the 1960's. Most of
this public money, however, goes into primary education which is
virtually all public and which is compulsory. Table 5-2 spells out
this tendency for four recent years. As was noted previously, educational services take up about ten percent of the total federal
(functional) budget.

Primary schooling takes by far the largest share of the education
budget, universities the smallest share. The necessity of this kind of
allocation is easy to understand in light of this Chapter and Chapter
Two's explanation of population trends, and one can expect that
there will be a continuing need for a similar allocation given the
population projections for the 1970's. According to Benítez, the number of persons in the five-to-fourteen year age group will continue
to increase into the 1980's even though their rate of growth may be
falling.[54]

Table 5-2, however, includes only funds from the federal government; state funds should also be included. Since state expenditures
nationwide total some fifteen percent or so of Federal expenditures,
and in turn some 25 to 35 percent[55] of state expenditures go into primary and secondary schools, amounts are fairly significant compared

TABLE 5-2

TOTAL FEDERAL BUDGET ASSIGNED TO EDUCATION, 1968 THROUGH 1971

[Millions of pesos]

Year	Total federal budget	Amount assigned to education	%	Amounts assigned to: *					
				Primary	%	Secondary	%	Higher education	%
1968	$61,414	$5,950	9.7	$2,650	4.3	$ 857	1.4	$ 966	1.6
1969	66,096	6,727	10.1	3,074	4.7	1,069	1.6	1,044	1.6
1970	72,229	7,276	10.1	3,250	4.5	1,269	1.8	1,214	1.7
1971	79,656	7,852	9.8	3,481	4.4	1,528	1.9	1,258	1.6

* Totals do not include libraries, construction, or "other" services.

Source: Secretaría de Hacienda y Crédito Público, Ingresos Totales de la Federación Según su Origen y Aplicación Presupuestal de los Mismos según su Destino, 1968 through 1971 editions.

to Federal outlays. State funds come predominantely from sales taxes (thirty percent) and property taxes (about 35 percent). Income taxes only account for some two percent of revenues.

Local funds are much less important. Except for the Federal District, which is more like a state in itself, municipalities generally lack a tax base, since all taxes including property taxes are preempted by other levels of government. Principal municipal incomes come from fees, licenses, fines, and other charges, and apportionments from the state governments.

The point of this discussion is that, unlike the U.S. where local and state governments predominate in primary and secondary education,[56] in Mexico it is the Federal Government which is most active. Under present conditions municipalities have little means of contributing to the educational effort, thus severely limiting one possible source of finance. If the Federal government were to increase its commitment to universities, without rearranging other priorities in order to continue its increasing support to primary schools, there would be a financial gap that would have to be filled by state governments. And state governments tend to rely on income-inelastic revenue sources, as listed above, limiting their growth over time.

However, amidst all this pessimism with regard to government philanthropy toward private universities, there are a few possibilities of government cooperation with the universities that should not be overlooked. Mexico has had a long tradition of governmental relationships with the private entrepreneur. Some authors would maintain that this relationship is a cooperative one. Eastin Nelson has written that " . . . Mexico is almost anarchical in the freedom to acquire riches which it accords men."[57] This kind of attitude is what Benjamin Higgins talks about when he writes of the "harmonious partnership" between government and business, the Mexican development "model" he credits with being responsible for the burgeoning of the Mexican economy.[58]

However, the spirit of encouragement of free enterprise has not been applied to education for reasons outlined earlier, and it is time that the Mexican government recognizes the public value of the private university, particularly in the growth situation that confronts education in the country. This kind of posture is more fitting to the needs and traditions of the society than the present one. Despite the limitations of public finance discussed above, there are ways that the Mexican government can assist the higher education industry.

One possible way has been presented above, tuition loans to students. Another is loans to the private institutions themselves, a practice which the Mexican government has followed for years in other growth industries. For example, Nacional Financiera, S.A., the country's principal credit organism, invested about 16.5 billion dollars in the national economy between 1965 and 1970. Of that total most went into physical infrastructure, but over four billion dollars was invested in public and private firms in basic and transformation industries.[59] If these kinds of firms are considered to have a net positive social return for a developing country, then why not educational firms, private as well as public, proprietary as well as non-profit?

Of course, some educational firms may not want to borrow, or to "mortgage their autonomy" as one university respondent put it in an interview. Because of the inherent difficulty for the large multi-university to meet its costs, i.e., to internalize the externalities of its product, many loans made in the higher education industry will probably have low or negative private returns. Yet this is precisely the area in which Nacional Financiera (NAFINSA) is constituted to operate — where social returns are high even though private returns may be low. For example, in 1970, 71 percent of NAFINSA's loans were made for public works, mainly electricity and irrigation. The share of NAFINSA funds devoted to physical infrastructure has increased steadily over the decade, from a base figure of 36 percent in 1960. It is highly unlikely that NAFINSA would involve itself in the development of educational resources, which function has been reserved to the Secretaría de Educación Pública. However, some public agency should place the same emphasis on the development of human capital that NAFINSA has put on physical capital.

It should be mentioned, however, that it is not absolutely necessary that a large successful university run at a loss. The Autonomous

University of Guadalajara is a case study which illustrates this point. Willing but unable inside Mexico to borrow seed money to build its new campus, the UAG was forced to look outside the country for assistance. That assistance came in the form of a U.S. Agency for International Development (AID) loan for some three million dollars, which the UAG was then able to triple using its own resources. Now the University is able to repay the loan, and in addition, is looking for other loans to finance new projects. The UAG case may be unique because of the institution's good fortune in attracting tuition-inelastic U.S. medical students into its student body. But the University is run by a very resourceful group of people, as are other private universities throughout the country, and it is probable that they would have found ways to meet their loan payments in any case.

Another possibility for government cooperation with the private universities is through public land grants. Mexico was never able to take advantage of the U.S. idea of the Morrill Acts that established many universities and endowed many others across the United States in the 19th Century.[60] Perhaps these grants were not appropriate for Mexico because of the way in which the country was settled and because of the low-value, poor-quality of most of its lands.[61]

However, Mexico did experience a thoroughgoing land reform movement as a result of its (20th Century) Revolution. The reform separated much formerly *hacienda* land into communal farms or *ejidos,* as part of Mexico's drive into the modern economy.[62] Distribution of land under the *ejido* movement has been virtually complete for some time now, but recently the Mexican government has been repurchasing or reclaiming unusable or unused *ejido* land, particularly along the western coastline, for development of tourist facilities. Tourism is one of Mexico's largest export industries, and both public and private development projects to expand tourism are in full swing. Since land grants are made for the benefit of the tourist industry, it would seem reasonable that they also be made for the higher education industry, particularly for those cases in which the grant would be associated with a university development project.

In short, there are many ways that the Mexican government could assist private (and even public) universities without going against its tradition and without rearranging its priorities with respect to school finance. Many possibilities for development of a nexus between the public and private sectors are open.

Auxiliary Enterprises: Possibilities

It has been the goal of many universities to obtain an integrated campus. Some universities, particularly UNAM, that have had such a campus, have experienced difficulties, and consequently many universities have become less enthusiastic than previously about having their own comprehensive campuses. Even if the barriers of budget and tradition were overcome, it is not clear now that integrated facilities would be built. For example, the new national university that is new being completed, the Autonomous Metropolitan University, (Universidad Autónoma Metropolitana — UAM) will not have a single campus, but several semi-autonomous units in different parts of the city.

An integrated campus, is, of course, not a necessary or sufficient condition for the programming of auxiliary enterprises. For example, the UAG completed in 1970 a new campus on the western side of Guadalajara which does not include dormitories. Mindful of the very real possibility of problems[63] when students are agglomerated, the university opted for a daytime campus of the community college type. However, the university does maintain a few of the common student service facilities such as the bookstore and the cafeteria, which it runs as small enterprises.

It is also quite possible, of course, for a university to operate associated enterprises quite apart from its educational facilities, as is the case with several institutions in the U.S. George Washington University, for example, has some prime real estate in Washington, D.C., along Pennsylvania Avenue which it leases to commercial firms. None of the Mexican universities that the author interviewed have been able to take advantage of such an arrangement.

One project which is still in the early stages of planning combines some aspects of both of the above possibilities, and thus deserves special mention. The UAG, as part of its second phase of development (the first phase being the recently completed 124-acre campus already referred to), has acquired by donation and purchase some one thousand acres of land to the northeast of the city. On this land the university plans to construct a new medical school and an associated medical services complex, with the possibility of including non-medical facilities to support the complex, such as housing of various types, commercial and recreational facilities, and even perhaps some light industrial enterprises that would coordinate with the environment. The name of the project is *"Ciudad Salud"* or "Health City," conveying the idea of a complete community constructed around medical-educational facilities.

The basic economic planning of *Ciudad Salud* was a project of the Business and Economics Research Center of the University, in which the author was involved. A model of community development was constructed,[64] similar to those developed for other communities in growth situations,[65] which proposed to analyze income flows between and among the medical and non-medical sectors. Initial suppositions for the model were these: that the medical student body would grow to some five thousand students, including the present ratio of U.S. students, that housing would be provided for students and for some three hundred and fifty families in addition, and that there would be sufficient commercial facilities for the community, including a hospital. Preliminary results of a run of the simulation model, using parameter estimates generated by current operational realities, indicate that the net private return to investment in *Ciudad Salud* would be respectable without taking account of any social return to the education and medical facilities. Depending on the size of the community (particularly non-students) and other considerations, the subsidy to the university could run from 2.5 million dollars to 10.6 million dollars for a net rate of return on investment of 4.3 percent to 10.6 percent.[66]

It goes without saying that this kind of enterprise requires a great deal of planning and coordination, and above all, management; but the return is considerable, not only to the society in terms of medical services and resources produced, but also to the university itself. Moreover, if the UAG builds such a facility without providing *any* revenue-raising community activities, it can expect to lose some three million dollars in annual subsidies to itself, resulting in a nearly break-even situation, provided that the U.S. students, from whom the UAG receives a substantial dollar subsidy, continue at present enrollment levels.

The UAG situation is based upon a private land grant which gives it the possibility of developing its facilities and, of course, more fund raising is necessary to provide the building capital. In this particular case, UAG is seeking loans from international organizations. Substantial donations and the use of its own funds will also be necessary. But the basic "capital" is the land itself, against which money can be raised. Success in the use of capital in a private sense, i.e., in providing a set of facilities that give a positive private return, depends upon the development of the land in a way that coordinates educational and medical plant with support facilities that generate revenue for the university.

This approach should be possible at other universities, private ones especially because of the entrepreneurial approach required. Unfortunately, few universities have the means or the good fortune to be able to acquire land for building purposes, particularly enough of it to make a community like *Ciudad Salud* posible. However, if the universities were able to obtain land grants, either through private charitable bequests, or from persons interested in raising the value of surrounding land in a developing suburban area, or from government, then the technique might be followed.[67]

What are the possibilities of generating revenues for the private universities from this source? It is this writer's opinion that of the non-tuition income sources, the development of auxiliary enterprises may be one of the most viable and, importantly, one of the most reliable consistent sources of revenues open to the Mexican private universities. It is also the most fitting with regard to the ability of the public sector to contribute to the private effort, and more in tune with the desire of many universities to retain their autonomy while yet meeting fast-growing budgets. There would be problems, to be sure, in planning; such enterprises may be risky ventures and universities may be too important to the society to assume the risk.[68] But returns can also be high, and it may be possible to diversify the associated risk by developing projects less complex than *Ciudad Salud,* or projects separated from the university itself, as in the case of some of the U.S. universities discussed earlier in this chapter.

Conclusion

This chapter has attempted to present a glimpse of the future demand for higher education in Mexico, and how the private universities might relate to this demand. Mexico's college-age population will be growing rapidly in the next ten years, probably more rapidly than ever before, and certainly faster than the public universities can receive them. Private universities must help educate these young people, yet their costs and tuitions are also growing rapidly, perhaps more so than they "should" grow in order to include more students from lower-income families. The chapter, then, has looked at possibilities for making university incomes more elastic, attempting to learn from the United States experience. It would appear that the most viable set of possibilities revolve around some special applications of public and private cooperation, where public assistance counts on private organization and entrepreneurship. This kind of cooperation in higher education would be new to Mexico in education but would be consistent with the history of her overall economic development.

REFERENCES:

1 Secretaría de Industria y Comercio, *Anuario Estadístico de los Estados Unidos Mexicanos, 1970-1971,* Tabla 6.1, p. 219. This figure excludes expenditures by state and quasi-state firms. On a functional basis, the amount for "*Servicios Educativos y Culturales*" has run about eight to ten percent of the total federal budget in the last several years.

2 For 1950 see Raúl Benítez Zenteno, *Análisis Demográfico de México,* 1969, pp. 108-9; for 1960 and 1970, Secretaría de Industria y Comercio, *VIII y IX Censo General de Población, passim."*

3 Asociación Nacional de Universidades e Institutos de Enseñanza Superior, *La Enseñanza Superior en México, 1966,* p. 31.

4 Actually, the national figure should be higher since the associated universities comprehend only some 84 percent of all university students. However, data on total university enrollment at all levels is not available for 1960.

5 ANUIES, *La Enseñanza Superior en México, 1970,* p. 19.

6 Raúl Benítez Zenteno, *op. cit., passim,* especially Appendix D.

7 For reference, in the U.S. for 1970, school enrollment was 47.7 percent for eighteen and nineteen year olds and 21.5 percent for the twenty-to-24 age group. (U.S. Department of Commerce, *Statistical Abstract of the United States, 1971,* p. 105).

8 *Ibid.,* p. 104-5.

9 In May 1973, 2000 students were refused entrance to the UNAM medical school because of lack of space and the low entrance examination results of the aspirants. The rejected students took possession of the Mental Health building and demanded admission. Finally after several days of negotiation, some of the students were admited notwithstanding the protests of the officials of the medical school who insisted that the resulting overcrowding would prejudice the quality of instruction. Such is the power of the Mexican idea of the "right" to education, even at the professional level.

10 Assuming that incomes of the universities equal the expenditures. Either because of careless reporting or because of non-balance accounting procedures, this is close but not necessarily exactly true in the ANUIES data.

11 By adjusting out the consumer price index increases for Mexico City, 1960 to 1970.

12 The six institutions were: Autonomous University of Guadalajara, Monterrey Technological Institute, Technological University of Mexico, Autonomous Technological Institute of Mexico, Iberoamerican University, Higher Institute for Comercial Studies.

13 Secretaría de Industria y Comercio, *Anuario Estadístico de los Estados Unidos Mexicanos, 1962-63,* p. 249, *1970-71,* p. 290.

14 U.S. Department of Commerce, *op. cit.,* p. 126.

15 In the U.S., public universities have been growing considerably faster than private ones. In the post-war period from 1947 to 1973, public enrollments grew about 450 percent while private enrollments increased only about 80 percent. (See U.S. Department of Health, Education, and Welfare, *Digest of Educational Statistics, 1973,* 1974, p. 74.)

16 Technological University of Mexico, Autonomous Technological Institute of Mexico, Iberoamerican University, Higher Institute for Commercial Studies, Aná-

huac University, Monterrey Technological Institute, Autonomous University of Guadalajara.

17   William G. Bowen, *The Economics of the Major Private Universities*, 1968, p. 35.

18   By contrast, at one of the most important of the Mexican institutions, Monterrey Technological Institute, the percent of income received in tuitions has *increased* in recent years — from 84 percent in 1969 to 91 percent in 1972.

19   These institutions reported their tuitions to ANUIES for 1968 and to the author in 1972. They were the six of the seven who reported reliance on tuitions earlier plus La Salle University, Women's University, and the School of Banking and Commerce. Accurate cost data for all the universities with which to compare these increases are not available for a longer period of time.

20   William G. Brown, *op. cit.*, p. 35.

21   *Sociedades "civiles"* or *"anónimas"* as they were called in Chapter Four.

22   Of the six sample institutions for cost and income data, one was a proprietary organization, the Higher Institute for Commercial Studies. This institution, as might be expected, receives no gifts.

23   There were three exceptions to this rule: the Colegio de México, an exception to nearly every rule in Mexican higher education, received 16 percent of its income from non-government gifts. The Autonomous University of Zacatecas for the first time in 1970-71 reported donations from "national foundations" that amounted to 25 percent of incomes. Finally, the University of the Southeast in Campeche reported a handsome subsidy from regional shrimp producers that amounted to 32 percent of its budget. However, this same subsidy amount, and exactly the same income figures overall, were reported for three years running by the University. (ANUIES, *op. cit.*, pp. 284ff.)

24   Sample of 231 universities. See Brakeley, John Price Jones, Inc., *Voluntary Support for Public Higher Education*, 1972, pp. 16-21.

25   Stromberg, *Philanthropic Foundations in Latin America*, 1968, pp. 131ff. Eight of the nine reported. The organization not listing financial data was the Mary Street Jenkins Foundation, one of the most important.

26   Again, public *member* universities of ANUIES are used as a proxy. These are the 33 largest public universities in the Republic. No public university with more than 2,000 students is excluded from this group. See ANUIES, *op. cit., 1971*, pp. 263ff.

27   One other university in the ANUIES data, a small (400 students) agricultural college in Ciudad Juarez, Chihuahua, receives government payment for tuitions of Federally sponsored students. Monterrey Technological also has a few of these students. See ANUIES, *op. cit., 1971*, p. 284.

28   William Bowen, *op. cit.*, p. 35.

29   In Chapter Two it was pointed out that this conflict finally resulted in the cessation of all Catholic Church services for three years in the 1920's.

30   Religious also teach in non-church private and even in public schools. For these reasons the distinction of a genre of universities based on religious affiliation is not analytically very helpful in Mexico.

31   Carlos Alvear Acevedo, *La Educación y la Ley*, 1963, p. 259. This idea finally formalized under the *Ley Orgánica de Educación*, promulgated in 1939.

32   From General Calles' address in Guadalajara in July 1934, quoted in *Ibid.*, p. 255. A fallout of Calles' cry was the founding of the Universidad Autónoma de Guadalajara, which rejected the socialist-communist aspect of government education and for years had to fight for its existence. Even today the University retains a defensive posture with regard to radicalism even though it appears to have succeeded in its struggle for existence.

33   For a comprehensive review of the Parsons case, see James D. Koerner, *The Parsons College Bubble*, 1970.

34   Martin Carnoy, "Rates of Return to Schooling in Latin America," *Journal of Human Resources*, Summer 1967, p. 359ff.

35   See summary article by George Psacharopoulos, "Rates of Return to Investment in Education around the World," *Comparative Education Review*, Feb. 1972, pp. 54ff. Of the thirty country studies cited by Psacharopoulos, only three, Brazil, West Nigeria, and Ghana were reported to have rates of return higher than Mexico's.

36   The measurement of this point would be an interesting subject for research. Several years ago the Economic Research Center at the University of Nuevo León attempted to measure by questionnaire elasticities among parents of the student body. Unfortunately results were inconclusive since the parents apparently suspected that the research was being conducted in order to raise tuitions and very few responded. The results were never published. Nor has much been done elsewhere. In his 1970 edition of *Economics of Education, A Selected Annotated Bibliography*, p. 42, Mark Blaug was able to say that "There has been little interest in the price elasticity of demand for education . . ."

37   In Mexico City alone there are over twenty private universities, many of which are competing for the same types of students.

38   Mexico City prices. From Banco Nacional de México, *Indicadores Económicos*, November 1974.

39   From 1960 to 1970 the comparable rate was about 3.5 percent.

40   Ifigenia M. de Navarrete, "La Distribución del Ingreso en México: Tendencias y Perspectivas." In David Ibarra and others, *El Perfil de México en 1980*, 1972, pp. 44ff.

41   In 1973-74 some 3600 Mexican students were enrolled in U.S. universities, about 2200 as undergraduates. (Institute of International Education, *Open Doors 1974: Report on International Exchange*, pp. 16-17.)

42   Mrs. Navarrete finds that in about 1960, income concentration was higher in Mexico than in Argentina, Brazil, Colombia, El Salvador, Venezuela, Panama, and Costa Rica (*op. cit.*, p. 47, Gini coefficient = .55).

43 Milton Friedman and Simon Kuznets, *Income from Independent Professional Practice*, 1965, p. 90.

44 For a general summary of income-contingent loans and their advantages over ordinary loans in education, see D. Bruce Johnstone, *New Patterns for College Lending*, 1972, pp. 13ff. A more detailed discussion of specific possibilities under such a loan program can be found in Stephen P. Dresch, and Robert D. Goldberg, "Variable Term Loans for Higher Education: Analytics and Empirics," *The Annals of Economic and Social Measurement*, Jan. 1972, pp. 52-92. Also see Ford Foundation Studies in Income Contingent Loans for Higher Education, *Pay-As-You-Earn, Summary and Recommendations*, 1972.

45 Stephen Dresh and Robert Goldberg, *op. cit.*, pp. 90ff.

46 In addition to the private return to the individual referred to earlier, Carnoy estimates the social rate of return at about thirty percent for completion of fourteen--to-sixteen years of schooling, i.e., at the university level. Carnoy's "private" rate refers to the rate of return to expenditures by students and their families aside from tuition. The "social" rate includes this private cost as well as institutional expenditures, both public and private. See Martin Carnoy, *op. cit.*, pp. 361ff.

47 Preliminary findings from the Yale "tuition-postponement" plan, begun in 1971, indicate high acceptance of the plan. Nearly one-fourth of the college signed up for the plan in the first semester of operation. See D. Bruce Johnstone and others, "Student Attitudes Toward Income Contingent Loans," *National Association of Student Financial Aid Administrators*, March 1972, pp. 11-27.

48 CONACYT provides unsecured loans which may be partially or totally forgiven, depending on the post-study activities of the loanee. For example, if the student returns to full-time teaching or research in a Mexican university, for a time equal to his training, his loan is converted entirely to a grant. If he works for the public sector, half of his loan is forgiven, and if for a Mexican-majority-owned firm, thirty percent. Only if he works for a foreign-owned firm is his loan completely repayable.

49 However, the loanee needs a co-signer. Interest rates are currently about two percent.

50 Luis Garibay G. and Vicente Valle H., *Financiamiento de la Universidad*, 1973.

51 An interesting set of publications that could be adjusted to the Mexican situation are those dealing with the economic impact of a university on the community. For example, John Caffrey and Herbert Isaacs have set up a model in *Estimating the Impact of a College or University on the Local Economy*, 1971. This model was then used by James Selgas and others at the Harrisburg Area Community College with some rewarding results. (See *The Impact of the College on the Local Economy, Research Report No. 11*, 1973.

52 The Mary Street Jenkins Foundation has donated some $800,000 to the UAG over three recent years.

53 A low-yield estate tax did exist until 1962, when it was rescinded, presumably because it cost more to collect than it returned. See Roberto Anguiano Equihua, *Las Finanzas del Sector Público en México*, 1968, p. 275.

54 R. Benítez Z., *op. cit.,* p. 108-109.

55 Estimate of Roberto Anguiano Equihua, *op. cit.,* pp. 368-369. For background on the information in this paragraph, see Anguiano's Chapter 22.

56 State and local funds accounted for over ninety percent of U.S. primary and secondary school revenues in 1968. See U.S. Department of Commerce, *op. cit.,* p. 120.

57 Eastin Nelson, *The Economic Potential of Mexico 1970-1975,* 1959, p. 15.

58 Benjamin Higgins, *Economic Development,* 1968, p. 640ff.

59 Secretaría de Industria y Comercio, *Anuario Estadístico Compendiado, 1970,* p. 353.

60 For an excellent summary of land grant history in the U.S., see George N. Rainsford, *Congress and Higher Education in the Nineteenth Century,* 1972, especially Chapters 1, 3 and 7.

61 For background see, among others, Lesley B. Simpson, *Many Mexicos,* 1966.

62 For a summary of the *ejido* movement, with an efficiency analysis, see Norris C. Clement, *The Ejido in Mexico,* 1970, pp. 1-4 and pp. 8ff.

63 Very present in educator's minds are the 1968 student riots in Mexico City that shut down the UNAM for a couple of months and threatened to cancel the 1968 Olympics. Some fifty people were killed during those demonstrations and over two hundred were injured. Such is the strife and violence that student power can provoke in Mexico. For a short, vivid description of the 1968 riots see, J. Patrick McHenry, *A Short History of Mexico,* 1970, pp. 209ff.

64 This model became the heart of a doctoral dissertation by Jay E. April of the University of Colorado: *"Ciudad Salud," A Simulation Study of a Community to be Built Around a Health Center in Guadalajara, Jalisco, México,* 1972.

65 See Charles C. Slater, with Harold M. Riley and others, *Food Marketing in the Economic Development of Puerto Rico,* 1970, and *Market Processes in the Recife Area of Northeast Brazil,* 1969.

66 Jay E. April, *op. cit.,* especially Chapter Six.

67 The last decade has seen a spectacular increase in the value of the land around the UAG campus, in the neighborhood of some 6000 percent!

68 For example, ITESM's investment in dormitories is paying less handsomely now than previously. In the early 70's, student inscription in the dormitories had fallen to about half of peak in the 1960's, and net revenues were down accordingly.

VI : SUMMARY OF CONCLUSIONS
AND RECOMENDATIONS FOR FURTHER STUDY

ᢒ Probably the definitive sources on public-private sector relations in Mexico, and their role in the development of the
country, are the seminal works written in the 1960's by Raymond
Vernon.[1] The success of Mexican development largely results, Vernon
maintains, from a unique combination of public and private effort
where each sector has contributed to the building of production
capacity.

Although not all students of Mexican development would agree
with him, Benjamin Higgins carries the idea further, calling the
relationship between public and private sectors "a 'happy marriage'
of bureaucrats and entrepreneurs."[2] Vernon himself would probably argue that it is less of a marriage than a Galbraithian standoff
of countervailing power which has produced the high rate of Mexican growth.

However, neither of these descriptions fits the kind of relationship
that has existed over the years between public and private sectors in
education, particularly higher education. A major theme of this book
has been the public-private dichotomy that exists in that industry.
It is seen that the dichotomy results from a set of historical circum-
stances which turn around a rejection of Church control of an elitist
system of education in the 19th Century and a national experiment
with socialism in the early 20th Century.

A basic problem that arises out of this dichotomy is the fact that
the private universities are virtually ignored in terms of public (government) funding. Although private sector higher education is rather
small compared to the public sector, the private institutions are
quite important to the higher education effort because, among other
things, they represent a quality component. This study has detailed
some of the measures of the qualitative difference between public
and private universities, and it is suggested that much of the difference is understandable on economic grounds in terms of resource

allocation; even without public funding more financial resources are committed per student among the private institutions than among the public ones. Much of these additional funds, perhaps as much as sixty percent, find their way into the market for human resources and in that market they buy more teaching inputs. Moreover, in a milieu of part-time professors it is the private universities in general which are attempting to professionalize teaching careers by hiring more full-time professors and paying more to get them. Therefore, the hypothesis that follows is that the private university should not be ignored by government. To the contrary, their "publicness" should be recognized, and they should be publicly (including governmentally) assisted, particularly in light of the large demand for higher education that Mexico faces in the next decades.

The problem then becomes, given the importance of the private universities, how can they find the financing necessary to continue their quality approach and at the same time expand their enrollments to assist in meeting the growing demand for higher education in Mexico.

It is seen that private universities rely heavily on tuitions and not only receive little funding from public sources, but very little from outside private sources as well. Tuitions have increased rapidly in recent years to cover cost increases implicit in efforts to raise quality. There is some doubt that the private universities can continue to do this, especially on equity grounds; pricing out students of lower-income families and returning to a modern-day elitism is not consistent with the Mexican tradition of mass education. New sources of revenue must be found to complement tuitions, but the U.S. model of public and private cooperation with universities is severely constrained in Mexico. Constraints include a shortage of public funds for the finance of education and a growing need for more resources at the primary and secondary levels; the fact that large philanthropic foundations oriented toward higher education have not yet developed; and the lack of a tradition and a tax system which encourages private bequests.

Nevertheless, there are some practical possibilities, and the present study has attempted to review these in the context of the Mexican constraints. One possibility might be student loans, particularly income-contingent loans with variable payback. These loans might be funded by the universities themselves along the lines of the Duke or Yale University plans, or even better, publicly through a national student loan fund. Public sector cooperation might be more feasible if loans were available to all students without regard to university attended, that is, whether public or private.

Another possibility might be loans to the universities themselves, through the public development bank, or another quasi-public financial organization. This approach, although perhaps politically more difficult than loans to students, is nevertheless consistent with the use of public loan funds in infrastructure industries, which has been practiced in Mexico for some time.

Finally, as regards public sector assistance, a major benefit for the private universities, one which would cost government little or no budget allocation, would be land grants conditioned on the development of university projects. Considerable emphasis is currently being placed on the tourist industry. Given the large social return of higher education, some emphasis could be placed on making land available to educational enterprises as well. As an aside, this technique could also be used as a stimulant to help decentralize higher education since land for grant purposes would probably be chosen outside the central areas.

Another avenue which is suggested is more effective self-help among the private universities themselves. The universities could generally give more attention to raising funds from alumni, foundations, corporations, and individuals. From the experience of some universities, there is evidence that considerable returns can be expected in this area under a well-organized fund-raising program. A further interesting possibility lies in university auxiliary enterprises, taking advantage of public or private land grants that would give the university the ability to generate complementary income for itself. An aspect of a private land-grant approach which has been discovered by at least two Mexican universities is the possibility of the universities' generating increased land values around the site so that the donors of the site, having conserved some land for themselves, could capture some benefits at the same time as they contribute to university development.

Much research remains to be done on the problem areas identified in this study. Attempts should be made to specify further the quality variables in Mexican education. The analysis herein presented comes close to assuming that more professors and a greater number of full-time professors mean better education. Although this may be true at the margin in Mexico, it certainly cannot be a viable long-run principle. Other variables must be important, of course, such as the qualifications of instructors. A whole area of fruitful study would be the better identification of training (and the academic degrees) appropriate to the Mexican universities at their present stage of development. It is not clear, for example, that the doctorate represents an appropriate degree program for aspiring university teachers in many fields for many Mexican universities.

Moreover, it may be that the private universities tend to produce a quality product because of the quality of the students they accept, i.e., those who have also had expensive pre-training; this proposition needs further testing. Also the fact that the private universities have more control over their students and their faculty and can exact an element of discipline that the public universities cannot may well be a critical consideration which should be subjected to better documentation. Lastly, it may be that in Mexico an entrepreneurial approach to education results in a more efficient use of the resources at hand so that the overall organization permits a better learning environment. All the above need to be investigated further in order to understand better the structure of education in Mexico, identifying strengths and weaknesses in that structure. It should be noted that most of these questions are not reducible to economic ones; so a multidisciplinary approach is required.

More areas are open for investigation around a basic problem herein examined: the financing of the private university. Much of the work which is necessary here is the definition of strategies as to opening up sources of funds, public and private, to the private universities. Careful analysis of each of the possible solution areas suggested here is essential to designing an overall approach to the successful financing of the private institutions. In particular, a study of loan possibilities to students and universities and the mechanism of such programs should be undertaken on a first priority basis. Next in order would be a study among Mexican firms with a view to identifying areas of possible cooperation with and donation to universities. A study of Mexican tax laws with reference to gift and/or bequest possibilities would also be most helpful, and not the least important would be an economic analysis of auxiliary enterprises among the U.S. universities to derive suggested plans relevant to the Mexican situation.

The writer would maintain, however, that the major thrust of assistance for higher education must still come from the public sector, given the kinds of educational demands that population pressure is putting on all Mexican institutions of higher learning. The central question that needs to be asked is what additional forms of public assistance are viable in the Mexican setting, and how can the government more rapidly come to address these opportunities? And, in the process, how can the dichotomy between public and private sectors which is no longer appropriate to the Mexican reality begin to be dissolved?

Raymond Vernon has written that, during the early years of Mexican development:[3]

... the Mexican governments responded in ways which were relevant to the needs of the Mexican people and in ways which supplemented the activities of the private sector instead of conflicting with them.

The same kind of expansive and pragmatic approach to development needs to be applied to higher education in Mexico in the coming years so that the country may produce the human resource inputs it urgently needs for continued growth.

REFERENCES :

1 Raymond Vernon, *The Dilemma of Mexico's Development: The Roles of the Public and Private Sectors,* 1963; and Raymond Vernon, ed., *Public Policy and Private Enterprise in Mexico,* 1964.

2 Benjamin Higgins, *Economic Development,* 1968, p. 642.

3 Raymond Vernon, *op. cit.,* 1963, p. 178.

BIBLIOGRAPHY

BOOKS

Academic Media, *Standard Education Almanac*, 1972, Orange, New Jersey.

Alegría, Paula, *La Educación en México Antes y Después de la Conquista*, 1936, Mexico City, Editorial "Cultura."

Almazán, Marco, *El Rediezcubrimiento de México*, 1970, Mexico City, Organización Navarro, S.A.

Alvear Acevedo, Carlos, *La Educación y la Ley*, 1963, Mexico City, Editorial JUS, S.A.

Anguiano Equihua, Roberto, *Las Finanzas del Sector Público en México*, 1968, UNAM, Textos Universitarios.

April, Jay E., *"Ciudad Salud": A Simulation Study of a Community to be Built Around a Health Center in Guadalajara, Jalisco, Mexico*, 1972, Boulder, Colorado, Doctoral thesis of the University of Colorado.

Asociación Nacional de Universidades e Institutos de Enseñanza Superior, *La Obra Educativa del Régimen del Presidente López Mateos, 1959-1964*, IV. *La Educación Superior*, 1964, Mexico City.

————, *La Enseñanza Superior en México, 1966* through *1971*, published 1969 through 1974, Mexico City.

————, *Directorio Nacional de Instituciones de Educación Superior*, Yearly, Mexico City.

Atcon, Rudolph, *The Latin American University*, 1966, Bogotá, ECO Revista de la Cultura del Occidente.

Balán, Jorge, Harley L. Browning, and Elizabeth Jelin, *Men in a Developing Society*, 1973, Austin, Texas, University of Texas Press.

Basave Fernández del Valle, Agustín, *Ser y Que Hacer de la Universidad*, 1971, Monterrey, Mexico, Centro de Estudios Humanísticos, Universidad de Nuevo León.

Benítez Zenteno, Raúl, *Análisis Demográfico de México*, 1961, Mexico City, UNAM Instituto de Investigaciones Sociales.

Benjamin, Harold R. W., *Higher Education in The American Republics*, 1964, New York, The McGraw-Hill Book Company.

Blaug, Mark, *Economics of Education: A Selected Annotated Bibliography*, 1970, New York, Pergamon Press.

———— ed., *Economics of Education*, 1968, Hammondsworth, England, Penguin Books.

Bowen, Howard R., *The Finance of Higher Education*, 1968, Berkeley, California, The Carnegie Commission on Higher Education.

Bowen, Howard R. and Paul Servelle, *Who Benefits from Higher Education and Who Should Pay?*, 1972, Washington D.C., American Association for Higher Education.

Bowen, William G. *The Economics of the Major Private Universities*, 1968, Berkeley, California, The Carnegie Commission on Higher Education.

Brakeley, John Price Jones, Inc., *Voluntary Support for Public Higher Education*, 1972, New York.

Bravo Ugarte, José, *La Educación en México*, 1966, Mexico City, Editorial JUS, S.A.

Brubacher, John S., *A History of the Problems of Education*, 1966, New York, McGraw-Hill Book Company.

Caffrey, John and Herbert H. Isaacs, *Estimating the Impact of a College or University on the Local Economy*, 1971, Washington, D.C., American Council on Education.

California and Western Conference, *Cost and Statistical Study, For the Year 1954-55*, 1956, Berkeley, California, California University Printing Department.

Calkins, R. N., *The Unit-Costs of Programs in Higher Education*, 1963, New York, Doctoral thesis of Columbia University.

Carnegie Commission on Higher Education, *The Capitol and the Campus: State Responsibility for Post-secondary Education*, 1971, New York, McGraw-Hill Book Company.

Cartter, Allan M. and others, *The Economics of Higher Education*, 1967, Princeton, New Jersey, College Entrance Examination Board.

Centro de Estudios Económicos del Sector Privado, A.C., *Análisis de la Potencialidad Económica del Area Metropolitana*, 1970, Mexico City.

Centro de Estudios Educativos, A.C., *Diagnóstico Educativo Nacional*, 1964, Mexico City, Textos Universitarios, S.A.

Centro de Investigaciones Económicas y de Negocios, *Reporte Dos: Médicos en México, Preliminar*, 1971, Guadalajara, México, Universidad Autónoma de Guadalajara.

Chambers, M. M., *Financing Higher Education*, 1963, Washington, D.C., The Center for Applied Research in Education, Inc.

Cheit, Earl F., *The New Depression in Higher Education*, 1971, New York, McGraw-Hill Book Company.

————, *The New Depression in Higher Education — Two Years Later*, 1973, Berkeley, California, The Carnegie Commission on Higher Education.

Clement, Norris C., *The Ejido in Mexico* (Research Monograph II), 1970, Boulder, Colorado, International Economic Studies Center of the University of Colorado.

Connery, Robert H., ed., *The Corporation and the Campus*, 1970, New York, Columbia University.

Derisi, Octavio Nicolás, *Naturaleza y Vida de la Universidad,* 1969, Buenos Aires, Eudeba.

Fagg, John Edwin, *Latin America, A General History,* 1963, New York, The Macmillan Company.

Ford Foundation Studies in Income Contingent Loans for Higher Education, *Pay-as-You-Earn, Summary Report and Recommendations,* 1972, New York, Ford Foundation.

Friedman, Milton and Simon Kuznets, *Income From Independent Professional Practice,* 1945, New York, National Bureau of Economic Research.

Froomkin, Joseph, *Aspirations, Enrollments, and Resources,* 1970, Washington, D.C., U.S. Office of Education.

Garibay G., Luis and Vicente Valle H., *Financiamiento de la Universidad,* 1973, Guadalajara, Mexico, Universidad Autónoma de Guadalajara.

Gill, Clark C., *Education in a Changing Mexico,* 1969, Washington, D.C., U. S. Department of Health, Education, and Welfare.

González Avelar, Miguel and Leoncio Lara Sáenz, *Legislación Mexicana de la Enseñanza Superior,* 1969, Mexico City, UNAM Instituto de Investigaciones Jurídicas.

Hansen, Roger D., *The Politics of Mexican Development,* 1971, Baltimore, Maryland, The Johns Hopkins Press.

Harbison, Frederick and Charles A. Myers, *Education, Manpower, and Economic Growth: Strategies of Human Resource Development,* 1964, McGraw-Hill Book Company.

Harris, Seymour E., *Higher Education: Resources and Finance,* 1962, New York, McGraw-Hill Book Company.

Haskins, Charles Homer, *The Rise of Universities,* 1923, Ithaca, New York, Cornel University Press.

Henke, Emerson O., *Accounting for Nonprofit Organizations,* 1966, Belmont, California, Wadsworth Publishing Company.

Higgins, Benjamin, *Economic Development,* 1968, New York, W. W. Norton & Company, Inc.

Innes, Jon T. and Others, *The Economic Returns to Education,* 1965, Eugene, Oregon, University of Oregon Press.

Institute of International Education, *Open Doors, 1974,* 1975, New York.

Johnston, Marjorie, *Education in Mexico,* 1956, Washington, D.C., U.S. Department of Health, Education and Welfare.

Johnstone, D. Bruce, *New Patterns of College Lending,* 1972, New York, Columbia University Press.

King, Richard, *The Provincial Universities of Mexico*, 1971, New York, Praeger Publishers.

Koerner, James D., *The Parsons College Bubble*, 1970, New York, Basic Books, Inc.

Larroyo, Francisco, *Historia Comparada de la Educación en México*, 1947, Mexico City, Editorial Porrua, S.A.

Latapí, Pablo, *Educación Nacional y Opinión Pública*, 1965, Mexico City, Centro de Estudios Educativos, A.C.

Levi, Julian H., and Sheldon Eliot Steinbach, *Patterns of Giving to Higher Education II*, 1972, Washington, D.C., American Council on Education.

López Cámara, Francisco, *El Desafío de la Clase Media*, 1971, Mexico City, Cuadernos de Joaquín Mortiz.

López Rosado, Diego G., *Problemas Económicos de México*, 1970, Mexico City, UNAM Textos Universitarios.

McHenry, C. Patrick, *A Short History of Mexico*, 1970, Garden City, New York, Doubleday & Company, Inc.

Millett, John D., *Financing Current Operations of American Higher Education*, 1972, Washington, D.C., Management Division, Academy for Educational Development, Inc.

Mushkin, Selma J., ed., *Economics of Higher Education*, 1962, Washington, D.C., United States Department of Health, Education and Welfare.

Myers, Charles Nash, *Education and National Development in Mexico*, 1965, Princeton, New Jersey, Princeton University.

Nelson, Eastin, *The Economic Potential of Mexico 1970-1975*, 1959, Santa Barbara, California, TEMPO.

Osborn, Thomas Noel II, *Public and Private Sector Higher Education in Mexico: An Analysis of Growth, Problems, and Opportunities*, 1973, Boulder, Colorado, Doctoral thesis of the University of Colorado.

Rainsford, George N., *Congress and Higher Education in the Nineteenth Century*, 1972, Knoxville, Tennessee, The University of Tennessee Press.

Reynolds, Clark W., *The Mexican Economy, Twentieth Century Structure and Growth*, 1970, New Haven, Connecticut, The Yale University Press.

Russell, John D. *The Finance of Higher Education*, 1964, Chicago, University of Chicago Press.

Sammartino, Peter, and Willis Rudy, eds., *The Private Urban University, a Colloquium*, 1966, Rutherford, New Jersey, The Farleigh Dickinson University Press.

Sánchez, George, *Mexico — A Revolution by Education*, 1936, New York, The Viking Press.

————, *The Development of Higher Education in Mexico*, 1944, New York, King's Crown Press.

Sánchez, Luis Alberto, *La Universidad Actual y la Rebelión Juvenil*, 1969, Buenos Aires, Editorial Losada, S. A.

Secretaría de Educación Pública, *Informe de Labores, 1971*, 1972, Mexico City.

Secretaría de Industria y Comercio, *Anuario Estadístico de los Estados Unidos Mexicanos, 1962-63* through *1970-71*, published 1964 through 1973, Mexico City, Dirección General de Estadística.

————, *IX Censo General de Población, 1970, Resumen General Abreviado*, 1971, Mexico City, Dirección General de Estadística.

Secretaría de Hacienda y Crédito Público, *Ingresos Totales de la Federación Según su Origen y Aplicación Presupuestal de los Mismos Según su Destino*, 1968 through 1971 editions, Mexico City.

Selgas, James W. and Others, *The Impact of the College on the Local Economy*, Research Report No. 11, 1973, Harrisburg, Pennsylvania, Harrisburg Area Community College.

Simpson, Lesley B., *Many Mexicos*, 1966, Berkeley, California, University of California Press.

Slater, Charles C., with Harold M. Riley and Others, *Market Processes in the Recife Area of Northeast Brazil*, 1969, East Lansing, Michigan, Latin American Studies Center, University of Michigan.

————, *Food Marketing in the Economic Development of Puerto Rico*, 1970, East Lansing, Michigan, Latin American Studies Center, University of Michigan.

Solis, Leopoldo, *La Realidad Económica Mexicana: Retrovisión y Perspectivas*, 1970, Mexico City, Siglo Veintiuno Editores, S. A.

Solmon, Lewis C., *Schooling and Subsequent Success: Influence of Ability, Background, and Formal Education*, 1973, Iowa City, Iowa, American College Testing Program (Research Report No. 57).

Stromberg, Ann, *Philanthropic Foundations in Latin America*, 1968, New York, Russell Sage Foundation.

Tax Foundation, Inc., *Public Financing of Higher Education*, 1966, New York.

UNESCO, *Statistical Yearbook, 1968* through *1971*, published 1969 through 1972, Paris.

————, *World Survey of Education*, 1971, Paris.

United Nations, *Demographic Yearbook, 1970* and *1971*, published 1971 and 1972, New York.

United States Department of Commerce, *Statistical Abstract of the United States, 1971*, Washington, D.C., Bureau of the Census.

U.S. Department of Health, Education and Welfare, *Digest of Educational Statistics, 1973,* 1974, Washington, D.C., Office of Education.

Vernon, Raymond, *The Dilemma of Mexico's Development, The Roles of The Private and Public Sectors,* 1963, Cambridge, Massachusetts, Harvard University Press.

————, ed., *Public Policy and Private Enterprise in Mexico,* 1964, Cambridge, Massachusetts, Harvard University Press.

Wolk, Ronald A., *Alternative Methods of Federal Funding for Higher Education,* 1968, Berkeley, California, The Carnegie Commission on the Future of Higher Education.

ARTICLES

Aguirre Beltrán, Gonzalo, "Organization and Structure of Latin American Universities," Report produced for Department of Educational Affairs, Pan American Union, Washington, D.C., 1961.

Bravo Ahúja, Víctor, "La Educación Técnica," in *Mexico, 50 Años de Revolución, IV. La Cultura,* 1963, Mexico City, Fondo de Cultura Económica.

Carnoy, Martin, "Rates of Return to Schooling in Latin America," *Journal of Human Resources,* Vol. II, No. 3, Summer 1967.

————, "Earnings and Schooling in Mexico," *Economic Development and Cultural Change,* Vol. 15, No. 4, July, 1967.

Castañeda, C. E., "The Beginnings of University Life in America," *Preliminary Studies of the Texas Catholic Historical Society,* Vol. III, No. 7, November 1940 (also in *The American Historical Review,* Vol. XX, No. 4, November, 1940.)

Dresch, Stephen P. and Robert D. Goldberg, "Variable Term Loans for Higher Education: Analytics and Empirics," *The Annals of Economic and Social Measurement,* Vol. 1, January, 1972.

Flores de la Peña, Horacio, "La Educación Superior y la Investigación Científica", in Manuel Bravo Jiménez and Others, *El Perfil de México en 1980,* Vol. 2, 1972, Mexico City, Siglo Veintiuno Editores, S. A.

Galper, Harvey and Robert M. Dunn, Jr., "A Short-Run Demand Function for Higher Education in the United States," *Journal of Political Economy,* Vol. 77, No. 5, September/October, 1969.

Gibson, Cyrus F., "The Development of Managers in Mexico — Report of a Survey," Ford Foundation study, mimeographed, January 1968. Published in Spanish as "La Preparación de Gerentes en México," *Contabilidad y Administración,* No. 47, June 1968, pp. 5 - 30.

Johnstone, D. Bruce, "The Role of Income Contingent Loans in Financing Higher Education," *Educational Record,* Vol. 53, No. 2, Spring 1972.

Johnstone, D. Bruce and Others, "Student Attitudes Toward Income Contingent Loans," *National Association of Student Financial Aid Administrators*, Vol. 2, No. 1, March, 1972.

Migoya, Francisco, "Universidad Iberoamericana, Mexico: The Ongoing Reform," in W. Roy Niblett and R. Freeman Butts, eds., *Universities Facing the Future*, 1972, San Francisco, California, Jossey-Bass, Inc.

Muñoz Ledo, Porfirio, "La Educación Superior," in *Mexico, 50 Años de Revolución, IV. La Cultura*, 1963, Mexico City, Fondo de Cultura Económica.

de Navarrete, Ifigenia M., "La Distribución del Ingreso en México: Tendencias y Perspectivas," in David Ibarra and Others, *El Perfil de México en 1980*, Vol. I, 1972, Mexico City, Siglo Veintiuno Editores, S. A.

Psacharopoulos, George, "Rates of Return to Investment in Education Around the World," *Comparative Education Review*, Vol. 16, No. 1, February, 1972.

Radner, R., and L. S. Miller, "Demand and Supply in U. S. Higher Education: A Progress Report," *American Economic Review, Papers and Proceedings*, Vol. 60, No. 2, May, 1970.

Roose, Kenneth, Charles C. Collins, and Rodney J. Morrison, "Financing Higher Education: Three Proposals," *Educational Record*, Vol. 51, No. 4, Fall, 1970.

Sanders, Thomas G., "The Church in Latin America," *Foreign Affairs*, Vol. 48, No. 2, January, 1970.

Waggoner, Barbara and Others, "Higher Education in Contemporary Central America," *Journal of Inter-American Studies*, Vol. VI, No. 4, October, 1964.

Waggoner, George R., "Problems in the Professionalization of the University Teaching Career in Central America," *Journal of Inter-American Studies*, Vol. VIII, No. 2, April, 1966.

APPENDIX A

CENTRO INTERNACIONAL
DE ESTUDIOS ECONOMICOS
Apartado Postal 32-214
Guadalajara 6, Jal.

CUESTIONARIO SOBRE LA UNIVERSIDAD

Nombre de la
Institución _____

Nombre del encuestado: _____

Puesto desempeñado _____

El presente cuestionario está diseñado para describir algunas de las características del funcionamiento de su Universidad. Favor de contestar las preguntas en la manera más completa y cabal que pueda Ud. hacerlo. Si algunos de los datos son confidenciales, favor de indicarlo y no se hará ninguna referencia a ellos en relación a su Institución. De todas formas, los datos se van a manejar con la máxima discreción y, ya que el enfoque de este estudio es el marco general de las Universidades del país, los datos se presentarán en forma agregada y no se identificarán con una Institución particular.

DATOS APROXIMADOS SON REQUERIDOS EN TODO EL CUESTIONARIO

1. ¿En cuales carreras se otorgan títulos profesionales?

Carrera	No. actual de estudiantes	No. de graduados 1971 u otro año	Fecha de iniciación de la carrera	No. actual de profesores		
				Tiempo Completo	Medio tiempo	Por hora

2. ¿Tienen Uds. otros programas impartidos *sin* que se otorgue título profesional, excepto preparatorias y secundarias? (Favor de describirlos brevemente, incluya número actual de alumnos y fecha de iniciación.)

3. ¿Operan Uds. escuelas secundarias y/o preparatorias? (Explique por favor, e indique número actual de alumnos y fecha de iniciación del programa.)

4. ¿Estudios de postgrado?

Campo	No. Actual de estudiantes	Graduados 1971 u otro año	Fecha de iniciación	Título ofrecido

5. Número total de alumnos en los últimos cinco años (estudiantes de tiempo completo o equivalente) y número total de graduados a nivel de licenciatura:

	No. de alumnos	No. de graduados
1972-73		
1971-72		
1970-71		
1969-70		
1968-69		

6. Favor de describir los requisitos de admisión para alumnos en las diferentes carreras profesionales.

----

7. Indique de cuales Estados de la República o areas geográficas provienen sus alumnos.

----

8. Número total de profesores en los últimos cinco años:

	Tiempo completo	Medio tiempo	Por hora
1972-73			
1971-72			
1970-71			
1969-70			
1968-69			

9. ¿Cuántas horas promedio por semana imparten clase sus profesores:

de tiempo completo? _____

de medio tiempo? _____

10. De sus profesores contratados por hora (o tiempo parcial menos de medio tiempo) ¿cuántas horas en promedio por semana enseñan estos profesores?

----

11. ¿Cuántos de sus profesores actuales:

1. son pasantes sin tesis terminada? _____
2. tienen su Licenciatura? _____
3. tienen títulos de postgrado: _____

Maestría sin doctorado? _____

Doctorado? _____

12. ¿Cuál es el salario promedio *por mes* al comenzar de los profesores de:

    tiempo completo? _____

    medio tiempo?   _____

13. Para los profesores pagados por hora, ¿cuál es el pago usual por hora-clase? _____

14. *Gastos totales* de la Universidad, en los últimos cinco años:

    1972-73 (estimar) _____
    1971-72   _____
    1970-71   _____
    1969-70   _____
    1968-69   _____

15. ¿Cuáles son sus gastos anuales por concepto de: (favor de indicar cantidades en pesos mexicanos o en porcentajes).

    Indicar año: _____   % ó $

    1. Instrucción?   _____
    2. Administración?   _____
    3. Bibliotecas?   _____
    4. Investigación?   _____
    5. Becas y préstamos
        para alumnos?   _____
    6. Planta física?   _____
    7. Otros gastos? (explicar)   _____

    _____

16. ¿Han cambiado de importancia relativa los renglones de gastos de la pregunta anterior en los últimos cinco años?

    EXPLICAR _____

    _____

    _____

17. Ingresos totales de la Universidad en los últimos cinco años:

    1972 - 73 (estimar) _____
    1971 - 72   _____
    1970 - 71   _____
    1969 - 70   _____
    1968 - 69   _____

18. ¿Cuàles son sus ingresos anuales por concepto de: (Favor de indicar cantidades en pesos mexicanos o en porcentajes.)

Indicar año: _____

% ó $

_____

    1. Colegiaturas y cuotas de alumnos? _____

    2. Donativos? _____

    3. Ingresos de capital? _____

    4. Otras ventas? (explicar) _____

    5. Subsidios o pagos del gobierno Federal? _____

    6. Subsidios o pagos del gobierno Estatal? _____

    7. Otros ingresos? (explicar) _____

19. ¿Han cambiado de importancia relativa los renglones de ingresos de la pregunta anterior en los últimos cinco años?

EXPLICAR _____

_____

_____

NOTA: EN LAS SIGUIENTES PREGUNTAS, FAVOR DE CONTINUAR SU EXPLICACION EN OTRA HOJA EN CASO DE SER PRECISO.

20. ¿Prevee Ud. algunos cambios de importancia durante los próximos cinco años en las cantidades recibidas de la pregunta No. 18?

EXPLICAR _____

_____

_____

_____

21. ¿A cuánto ascienden sus colegiaturas actuales por semestre?

$_____MN (Si todos no son iguales para todos los alumnos, favor de indicar las diferencias.)

_____

_____

_____

_____

22. ¿Cuántos volúmenes contienen las bibliotecas dependientes de su Universidad?

_____

23. ¿Cuáles son los problemas económicos que Ud. prevee que su Institución tendrá en los próximos cinco años? (Favor de explicar brevemente.)

24. ¿Cuáles son los problemas *no*-económicos que Ud. prevee que su Institución tendrá en los próximos cinco años? (Favor de explicar brevemente.)

25. ¿Cree Ud. que problemas económicos de su Universidad en el futuro inmediato provocarán una reducción o limitación de sus programas educativos actuales, o una reducción en la *calidad* de los programas actuales? (Explicar brevemente).

26. ¿Qué cantidad o porcentaje de su presupuesto actual puede asignar su Universidad para el mejoramiento de sus programas educativos?

27. Si su Institución tiene algún programa de intercambio de alumnos con otra universidad dentro o fuera de la República, favor de describirlo brevemente:

----

28. ¿Puede Ud. describir los trabajos de investigación que se llevan a cabo actualmente en su Universidad?

QUEDAMOS MUY AGRADECIDOS
POR SU TIEMPO Y ESFUERZO

INDEX